Herbs, Useful Plants

Robert Eagle

British Broadcasting Corporation

This book is published in conjunction
with the BBC Radio series *Herbs, Useful Plants,*
first broadcast on Radio 4 in Autumn 1981

The series is produced by Jude Howells

The illustrations by Sue Henry,
on pages 40, 53, 59, 67 and 74,
were specially commissioned

The front and back cover photographs are
© Tessa Traegar
They are part of a poster specially
commissioned by the Herb Society
who have copies available for sale

The author would like to thank
Giancarla Forte for her patient assistance
and the designer of the book, Sally Grover

Published to accompany a series
of programmes prepared in consultation with the
BBC Continuing Education Advisory Council

First published 1981
Published by the British Broadcasting Corporation
35 Marylebone High Street, London W1 1AA

This book is set in 11/12 pt Garamond VIP
Printed in England by Mackays of Chatham Limited, Kent

ISBN 0 563 16497 2

Contents

The author

Robert Eagle is a broadcaster and journalist specialising in medical matters. He regularly contributes to the BBC, *Sunday Times*, *World Medicine* and many other national, scientific and medical publications. As a staff writer on the *General Practitioner* magazine he won the Lilly Medical Journalism Research Award in 1975. In 1979 he was awarded the Medical Journalists' Association prize for his first of several books on medical matters and has received this award again in 1981.

The author has written this book as a background to the BBC Radio series he presented. It contains additional material to the programmes, and features further interviews with herbalists, doctors, herb growers, cooks and cosmetologists, discussing every aspect of herbs and their use to mankind.

'Smelly Weeds'

When broadcasters want to get a little light relief into their programmes, they often resort to a stratagem known in the trade as the 'vox pop'. Short for *vox populi*, 'voice of the people', vox pops consist of brief interviews with passers-by (usually not a million miles from the environs of Broadcasting House) whom the reporter has managed to lure to the microphone. The snippets of comment and ribaldry which get broadcast are not generally expected to contribute vastly to the sum of human understanding on a subject, but they do help to lift the leaden atmosphere which is often created by the ponderous deliberations of experts. They are a crude but colourful kind of opinion poll.

So, before embarking on this book and the programmes which it accompanies, I ventured into the streets of the London postal district I inhabit, to ask people to tell me what they thought about herbs or, as I call them, 'useful plants'. Here are a few of the views I elicited:

'. . . *smelly weeds* . . .'
'. . . *pretty little plants for the rockery* . . .'
'. . . *what witches put in spells* . . .'
'. . . *useful for stuffing chickens with* . . .'
'. . . *nice in glass jars for decorating the kitchen* . . .'
'. . . *a thing of the past* . . .'

I got the general idea that most people (if it is reasonable to assume that a Saturday-afternoon vox pop on a busy high road can represent the views of most people) did not really take herbs very seriously. Those who admitted to knowing one end of a frying pan from the other agreed that herbs were good for cooking, though most of them got not much further than naming parsley, sage, rosemary and thyme, and seldom used more than one or two herbs in their kitchen. Most were sceptical of the claims made for 'healthy' herbal cosmetics. And those who had any views at all about herbal medicine thought that it was fifty-per-cent whimsy and fifty-per-cent quackery. Admittedly there was the occasional enthusiast who declared that all modern synthetic products were dreadful poisons and that natural products like herbs were *per se* healthy, safe and good for you in every way; but all in all, the consensus seemed to be that herbs were not really of much use or significance and largely, as the lady said, 'a thing of the past'.

Now, if broadcasting is supposed to give voice to the opinions of the people, I fear that the programmes I presented on herbs may be condemned as a dereliction of that duty, for the majority of individuals interviewed in those programmes had very different ideas about the importance of herbs. They took herbs very seriously, and some brandished words like 'ethnobiology', 'pharmacognosy' and 'transcultural anthropology' to demonstrate that the herbs they were talking about were not some bit of flim-flam in a rockery but a worthy subject of academic attention and financial investment.

These interviewees were not all rural escapologists or dug out from musty university herbaria. They included practical scientists, medical practitioners and – to show that the study of herbs could have pleasurable results – an agreeable garnish of cooks, bons viveurs and cosmetologists. The gist of their opinions was that herbs are useful and, despite the olde worlde associations that cling to the word 'herbs' like rotten ivy, they are very much a thing of the present and the future.

So what are herbs? For botanists the term 'herb' is a technical one meaning a plant with a soft stem (not the woody stems of shrubs and trees) which flourishes for only a short time above the ground. But 'herb' also has a more general meaning, which is the one I am adopting here. It is a plant, any plant, which has a special use for mankind – be it as a food, medicine, flavouring, colour, cosmetic, scent or fibre.

Plants are defined as herbs if we like or need them, and weeds if we don't. Many of the plants named as herbs in this book are shrubs or trees or grasses rather than the wild flowering annuals which botanists call herbs. So now that herbs have been defined for present purposes as 'useful plants', you should not be surprised to find familiar herbs like parsley, sage, rosemary and thyme cropping up in the unfamiliar company of cannabis, cocoa, deadly nightshade, foxgloves and hops.

Possibly the main reason that city dwellers in the Western world are now inclined to regard herbs as a thing of the past is that many of the substances which could once only be provided for us by plants have been replaced by synthetic, chemical alternatives. At the turn of the century more than ninety per cent of the medicines listed in the *British Pharmacopoeia* were derived directly from plants, whereas today probably less than ten per cent of the drugs doctors prescribe in the West are plant-based. Cotton, wool and silk are, of course, still worn, but they are luxury textiles in relation to the cheap synthetics like viscose, polyester and nylon. And how often do you enjoy a strawberry ice-cream flavoured with real strawberries? Even herbal essences like vanillin, which one might fondly believe, judging by its name, to be a plant extract, are now synthesised: the only plant material used for making the vanilla essence you find in supermarkets is wood pulp.

Nevertheless it is very easy for us, snug and drugged by our synthetic comforters, to overlook our utter dependence on plants. From one point of view all plants could be regarded as useful plants, because without plants the whole biological cycle of the world would stop turning. They are our food and the source of the air we breathe. They turn carbon dioxide and water and the inedible elements of the soil into oxygen for our lungs and proteins, vitamins and carbohydrates for our nourishment (or the nourishment of the animals we eat). And for people who still live in societies which have only been partially transformed by the Industrial Revolution (that is, most of the people of the world) plants are the main source of medicines, textiles, cosmetics and dyes. So, although some people may be tempted to laugh at the magic and mystery which informs a lot of herbal lore, they should not be surprised that their ancestors — and others who still recognise their debt to useful plants — should have regarded their herbs with such veneration.

This book isn't going to be a scholarly tome, but it isn't going to subscribe to the vox pop view of herbs either. If it has any purpose it is to point out that we may have forgotten a lot of valuable old knowledge about herbs and that our continuing neglect could deprive us of benefits untold.

Ancient Science and Modern Magic

'*Chemists, botanists and doctors are the direct descendants of the old alchemists, herbalists and magicians. The apparent successes of our modern technology may tempt us to believe that we know how to manipulate nature much better than they did. But our scientific philosophy and methods are barely more than a century old. We are Johnny-come-lately's and we have a great deal to learn about plants.*'

These words, from Dr Conrad Gorinsky, a research scientist at a London teaching hospital, whose work with plants will be described later on, might prove hard for his scientific colleagues to swallow. Admittedly, few would be rash enough to claim that they did not still have a great deal to learn: of the 300,000 or so plant species which have been identified so far, only a relative handful, about 10,000, have been investigated for their chemical or medicinal properties, and in most cases the examination has been very cursory. At the herbarium at Kew alone, for example, there are brief notes on several thousand plants deposited by botanists from all over the world which suggest that these plants may be useful as medicines. This information was collected by the botanists from their conversations with local people, but as yet no one has found the time or money to investigate these claims using contemporary scientific methods. Many scientists would object, however, to the suggestion that their methods are not superior to those of ancient magicians. The purpose of scientific method is objective assessment, to establish facts without being sidetracked by myth and prejudice.

The principles of contemporary science developed as a reaction against the religious and mystical attitudes which once dominated intellectual life. One of the great landmarks in the development of modern scientific thought was Darwin's arguments with the Church. Most Christian intellectuals in the early nineteenth century believed that the Bible explained the origin of species and that the Bible's explanation could not be questioned. Darwin argued that this was putting theory before the facts and that truth could be established only by observing nature in action.

Theories are, of course, only an approximation of the truth based on imperfect knowledge. We need them because without them we would feel that we were cast adrift in a baffling and meaningless world. They appeal to our sense of order. So although some of the theories which used to be advanced to explain mankind's relationship with nature may strike twentieth-century scientists as absurd, they too were based on observation and available knowledge.

The Four Elements

The old herbalists and magicians saw the world in a completely different way from a modern chemist. They had no idea that physical matter could be separated into thousands of different chemical entities. The basic elements of life which they observed were fire, air, earth and water, and they assumed that all matter must be made up of different combinations and proportions of these elements. Moreover, they generally assumed that there was some kind of life force or invisible energy which put nature into action.

In European literature the idea of the Four Elements found its first expression in the teachings of the Greek philosopher Empedocles and the medical writings of Hippocrates and his colleagues in the fifth century BC. These elements were manifested in the human body by four humours: blood, phlegm, yellow bile and black bile. Blood, like air, was hot and wet; phlegm, like water, was cold and wet; yellow bile, the caustic-tasting secretion of the liver, corresponded to fire, which is hot and dry; and black bile (which is not what we call bile, but a tarry substance found in the spleen made up of dead blood cells) was cold and dry like the earth. The physician's job was to ensure that the elements were kept in an equal, harmonious balance.

An illustration of the way in which Hippocrates saw the theory of the Four Elements at work in nature comes in the writing entitled *Of Airs, Waters and Places*. Hippocrates commented that people who live in hot, southern climates tend to be fat and indolent and, if they fell ill, commonly suffered from hot, bilious diseases like dysentery. People living in places exposed to the cold wet winds of the North, on the other hand, were more vulnerable to cold, wet diseases like pneumonia and rheumatism. He wrote:

> '*A climate which is always the same induces indolence but a changeable climate induces laborious exertions both of body and mind . . . changes arouse the understanding of men and do not allow them to become torpid.*'

Hippocrates' teachings did much to dispel the more primitive notions of sickness and health, which were basically that disease was caused by evil spirits lurking in the environment. Plants which could relieve the symptoms of disease were held in great awe because it was assumed that they housed benevolent spirits which could drive the evil ones away. Though the theory of the Four Elements may seem quaint today, it was an advance on this old animist theory and it flourished in Europe until the seventeenth century, and is still the basis of the Unani system of medicine which is practised in Pakistan, northern India and most parts of the Arab world today.

Ayurvedic medicine in southern India is based on a complicated hierarchy of forces which include three humours (wind, bile and phelgm) and five elements (earth, air, fire, water and ether). And in Chinese medicine too there are five elements – fire, air, earth, water and metal – which are animated by a vital force called *Chi*.

What has all this got to do with herbs? Well, just as the human body was seen to be influenced by an interplay of the elements or humours, plants too were subject to the same principles. For a Pakistani *hakim* (medical practitioner), for example, turmeric is a hot, dry herb which might be used to treat a cold, wet disease like diabetes. The same *hakim* would recommend that a healthy person should not eat a curry which contained a lot of hot pepper unless the pepper was balanced with 'cold' coriander. In Chinese medicine *The Barefoot Doctor's Manual* describes four types of constipation: hot, cold, gassy and bloody, each with its own remedy based on herbs with contrary properties. In European medicine we can see the old elemental theory at work in a traditional remedy for rheumatism which is still popular today, mustard baths. Mustard is, of course, a hot, dry herb and is therefore ideal for relieving a cold, wet complaint.

The Four Elements theory, like most theories, is a combination of shrewd observation and imaginative guesswork. In medicine it has always been rivalled by another school of thought which, on the face of it, seems to be diametrically opposed to it.

Sympathetic magic and the Doctrine of Signatures

In 1526 a large square near the university in Basle was thronged with a crowd watching a spectacle which had been laid on by the newly appointed professor of medicine. This gentleman, who rejoiced in the name of Philippus Aureolus Theophrastus Bombast von Hohenheim, had cleared the libraries of all the books by the two leading medical authorities of the day, Galen and Avicenna, and had ordered them to be burnt. This was a gesture which was to cost him dear, because it lost him his job and alienated the vast majority of contemporary physicians. Both Galen, a Greek, and Avicenna, an Arab, had died many centuries earlier, but very few doctors since their times had managed to compete with them in anatomical expertise and practical wisdom. Indeed, medicine had become such a stultified, fossilised subject that their teachings had almost acquired the status of Holy Writ, which few dared to question. As one might expect, however, they did have their faults, and von Hohenheim intended to make that plain.

Von Hohenheim is remembered today by the name he adopted several years later: Paracelsus. He was a scientist with a voracious appetite for learning. As well as being well enough versed in anatomy and physic to know that Galen had often got his anatomy wrong and that the drugs which Galen's followers dished out to their patients in generous quantities often caused more harm than good, Paracelsus had studied astrology, alchemy and 'the black art', necromancy. It was from these studies that he had picked up an idea which has always run through magic, the idea that power can be gained over someone or something through a plant or image which resembles that person or object.

Philippus Aureolus Theophrastus Paracelsus.

This power is called 'sympathetic magic'. A crude form of sympathetic magic is the doll which is dressed up to look like the intended victim and then stuck with pins. But sympathetic magic has another, positive aspect which is the one seen in herbal medicine. Ginseng root and mandrake root, for example, have been extolled as medicines for centuries. They both have potent medicinal properties – ginseng as a gentle stimulant and mandrake as a soporific – but the main reason why they have grabbed the imagination and gained a reputation as panaceas is that their roots often bear an uncanny resemblance to the shape of the human body. You may have noticed that, although the companies which market ginseng today give much prominence to the scientific research which has been made into the plant, their advertising material often displays a very humanoid-looking root: the image is still very compelling.

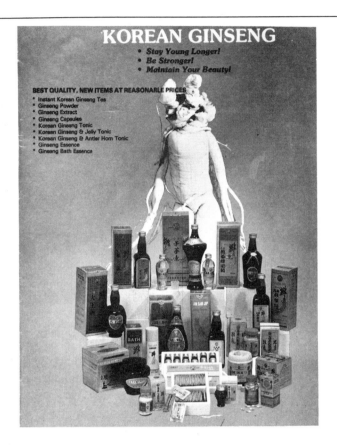

The Four Elements theory espoused by Hippocrates, Galen and Avicenna had suggested that diseases should be treated with medicines which had a contrary effect to the excessive humours. However, Paracelsus revived the notion that each herb had an individual 'signature' – in other words, that its shape, colour, location, and the time and manner of its growth offered clues about the medicinal uses it could be put to – as if the plant had a soul which was reflected in its outer form.

Woundwort, *Stachys sylvatica*, for example, contains a reddish juice which looks rather like blood. According to the Doctrine of Signatures, this would explain why it was good at staunching wounds. Parsley piert, *Aphanes arvensis*, used to be very popular with herbalists for treating bladder and kidney stones. Because it grows in gravel and stony ground, according to the Doctrine of Signatures this would explain why it was so efficient at breaking through stones in the body. Birthwort, *Aristolochia clematis*, has leaves which are shaped like a womb; hence, according to the Doctrine of Signatures, its usefulness as an aid to women in labour.

The sundew, *Drosera rotundifolia*, is a small plant which grows in marshland. Like the well-known Venus flytrap, it is an insectivorous plant, and it secretes a sticky liquid which it uses to attract and trap little insects. For the alchemists, however, this sticky liquid was a form of dew. As they regarded dew as the purest distillation of water, the sundew liquid, which never evaporated even at midday, was held to be an elixir of immortality and prescribed for longevity.

Two more examples of the Doctrine of Signatures in practice are the old belief that walnut kernels, which bear a strong resemblance to the shape of the brain, are therefore 'good for the brain'; and that the willow tree, *Salix*, which grows in damp places, was good for treating diseases associated with such areas, like rheumatism and 'the ague'. In fact, this last example suggests that there was more to the Doctrine of Signatures than mere whimsy; for willow bark is a source of salicylic acid, the chemical on which aspirin is based. Like aspirin, an infusion of powdered willow bark is undeniably effective against aches and fevers.

The idea of signatures is not confined to Europe and medicine. The Atharva Veda writings, which are the foundation of Ayurvedic medicine in India, claim that the lotus root, because of its yellow colour, is a cure for jaundice. The snakeroot, *Rauwolfia serpentina*, with its long, serpentine roots, was alleged to be a cure for snakebites. One wonders how many were cured.

Paracelsus and his followers extended the Doctrine of Signatures to speculative extremes. The Italian herbalist Gianbattista Porta even went as far as declaring that plants with short lives were hazardous because they would shorten the life of anyone who consumed them. Basil, *Ocimum basilicum*, apart from its excellence as a culinary herb, was seriously believed by seventeenth-century English herbalists like John Parkinson and Nicholas Culpeper to be a potentially evil, noxious herb which attracted scorpions. Indeed, it was widely believed at the time that if a basil plant was left under a pot it would turn into a scorpion. Despite their distrust of the plant, however, they recommended it for relieving insect bites and stings, basing their advice on the principle that the evil in the plant had a natural affinity for the venom. This is what Culpeper wrote:

> *'Being applied to the place bitten by venomous beasts or stung by*
> *a wasp or hornet, it speedily draws the poison to it. Every like*
> *draws its like.'*

Like Paracelsus, Culpeper was a student of astrology, and in his view all plants were under the influence of the heavenly bodies and all had star signs which defined their character. Marigolds, for example, were a 'herb of the Sun and under Leo. They strengthen the heart exceedingly and are very expulsive.'

The soporific poison in henbane revealed the herb to be under the lugubrious influence of Saturn:

> *'All herbs which delight most to grow in saturnine places are*
> *saturnine herbs. Henbane delights most to grow in saturnine*
> *places, and whole cartloads of it may be found near the places*
> *where they empty the common jakes and scarce a ditch to be found*
> *without it growing by. Ergo, it is a herb of Saturn.'*

Culpeper's herbal, *The English Physician*, was first published in 1653, and modern editions of the book are still available today. Many practising herbalists dislike Culpeper and resent his continuing influence. A minority of herbalists do still believe that interesting connections can be drawn between astrology, herbs and the Doctrine of Signatures, but most professionals like those who form the membership of the National Institute of Medical Herbalists are keen to re-establish herbalism on a contemporary scientific footing.

Homoeopathy

Nevertheless, the principles of sympathetic magic do live on in a branch of medicine which appears to be making a comeback of late – homoeopathy. The word 'homoeopathy' is derived from the Greek and means 'similar suffering', and homoeopathic principles are almost diametrically opposed to those of conventional medicine, which homoeopaths refer to as allopathy, 'different suffering'. The difference between homoeopathy and allopathy is really very similar to the difference between Paracelsus' idea that disease should be treated with 'similars' and Galen's approach based on 'contraries'.

Though the basic premise of 'like cures like' is almost as old as medicine itself, modern homoeopathy was the brain-child of Samuel Hahnemann, a physician, who was born in Meissen in 1755. Like all the physicians of his day Hahnemann had to rely largely on herbal medicines to treat his patients, and like Paracelsus he was alarmed and disgusted by the practices of many of his colleagues who gave their patients large doses of several medicines at once, the only effect of which was to make them even sicker than they would have been if they had received no treatment at all. One of Hahnemann's first experiments was to see how far he could reduce the dose of a medicine and still retain some therapeutic effect. In fact, he often ended up by giving his patients minute doses. This principle continues in homoeopathy today; homoeopathic remedies are prepared by diluting and shaking the medicines many times so that there is often only the barest trace, if any trace at all, of the original herb left. Homoeopaths say that these minute doses are not only effective, but can prove even more potent than large ones. This idea hardly conforms with orthodox pharmacology, and sceptics maintain that if patients do well on homoeopathic treatment it is simply because they have been taken off conventional drugs which were causing disagreeable side effects and are therefore almost bound to feel better – a criticism which does not reflect well on allopathy or homoeopathy! Others say that if homoeopathy works at all it is by suggestion, the fact that the patient believes in the doctor and the medicine that he or she prescribes. But this, too, is a view which can be equally applied to allopathy. Homoeopaths are a bit short of hard evidence which would persuade their critics that they are providing anything more effective than suggestion, though some formal clinical trials were recently completed by Glasgow doctors, the results of which do appear to indicate that homoeopathic treatment is more effective than suggestion. The trials, which were conducted on patients suffering from rheumatoid arthritis, also showed that homoeopathic treatment was better than aspirin, which is still one of the standard anti-inflammatory drugs used for treating arthritis.

However, let's leave these squabbles aside and look at the medicines which homoeopaths prescribe. Briefly, the main principle of homoeopathic prescription is that you give a patient a medicine which would give a healthy person similar symptoms if it was taken in a large enough dose. In other words, a herb which can cause symptoms if taken in excess will cure them if taken in very small amounts.

The classic examples of this principle in action which are always cited by homoeopaths are cinchona and belladonna, two of the medicines first investigated by Hahnemann himself. *Cinchona succirubra*, or Peruvian bark, was introduced to Europe in the seventeenth century by Jesuits who had found it being used by South American Indians against malaria. It is the source of quinine, which is still used to prevent and treat this disease. In order to acquire first-hand knowledge of the action of cinchona, Hahnemann tried it on himself and in a large dose. He found that overdosage put him into a state of fever and near delirium, which was just like the symptoms of the disease the drug was so good at relieving. Belladonna, he later discovered, had a similar effect; though it was used to treat scarlet fever, large doses of belladonna given to healthy volunteers provoked the signs and symptoms of that very disease.

Homoeopaths have several hundred herbal remedies in their repertory which they prescribe on this 'like cures like' premise. Rather than matching a particular drug to a particular disease, homoeopaths try to match the characteristics of a remedy – namely, the symptoms that it would provoke in a healthy person – to the patient's symptoms. One of their most frequently used remedies is aconitum, which comes from monkshood, *Aconitum napellus*. This plant is very poisonous, and the symptoms of poisoning are tingling and irritation of the skin and mucous membranes, restlessness and anxiety. A homoeopathic dose might be given to a child with croup. Alternatively, if you had a nasty cold and your symptoms included red, watery eyes, sneezing and an acrid discharge from your nose, you might well be prescribed *Allium cepa*, better known as the common onion.

I expect that many homoeopaths would resent being called practitioners of sympathetic magic, even though sympathetic magic has a long medical tradition. Some of what we might call the more laboratory-oriented homoeopaths have tried to demonstrate that their tiny doses do have a measurable physical effect on organisms in test tubes. But although some experiments have yielded the desired result, attempts to repeat them have generally ended unsuccessfully.

Anthroposophy

On the other hand there are a number of homoeopaths and a few allopaths who adopt the overtly mystical approach to medicine which was delineated by the Austrian mystic-cum-scientist Rudolf Steiner. Steiner's visionary philosophy – anthroposophy – embraced medicine, agriculture, architecture – indeed most areas of human endeavour – and it declared that all physical matter was formed and set into action by cosmic forces. Steiner drew complex correlations between man, plants and the minerals of the earth and their relationships with extra-terrestrial influences like the sun, moon and planets. He saw three principal forces at work in man, which were reflected in plants. Firstly there was the 'thinking' aspect of man, which Steiner associated with the brain, nerves and sensory organs. The 'feeling' aspect, concerned with spreading energies around the body and emotions, was centred on the chest with its heart, lungs and spreading network of blood vessels. The third aspect, which he called 'will', but which could perhaps equally well be described as instinct, centred on the abdomen, which houses the main metabolic organs and the reproductive ones.

Plants, Steiner believed, had a rather similar kind of structure, though with them it was the other way round. The roots, responsible for exploring the earth and searching for food, corresponded to the 'thinking' aspect in man. The leaves and stems, like the heart, lungs and arteries, were responsible for the flow of sap, while the flowers and fruit were associated with reproduction and regeneration. In terms of medical therapy what this all signified was that the practitioner should treat an aspect of the human body with a corresponding part of a plant. Digitalis leaf, for example, would be more effective than the flower or root for treating the heart. A headache remedy would come from the root of a plant, whereas fruit or flowers would have the greatest effect on hormone levels.

This is admittedly a very abbreviated account of Steiner's ideas about the relationship between man and plants; but I mention it briefly as an example of the way in which the ancient ideas of similars and signatures have continued to thrive and develop and throw up new variations.

Homoeopathy and anthroposophy were both thought out by high-minded individuals who regarded themselves first and foremost as scientists. For many scientists today their ideas may sound somewhat weird, mystic and unsubstantiated. They are perhaps out of tune with the post-Darwinian age in which science and religion have taken separate paths and are thought by a lot of people actually to be mutually incompatible. Scientists like to have material proof before they will believe in anything. Religions say that truth cannot be found by studying material things and that it is only glimpsed through inspiration and faith. Yet, for the old herbalists and alchemists, science and religion were closely related. They shamelessly combined mysticism and physical science, because, for them, both were means of explaining how we fitted into the world about us and the heavens above. They would have been appalled by the modern atheist notion that man is a bag of chemicals shuffled together by a combination of chance and blind instinct.

Witches' brews

If we delve further back into herbal lore we might expect to find that the associations between plants and the powers that they were ascribed were even less scientific. What should we make, for instance, of the old witches' brews made of herbs and toads which were supposed to make you take off on your broomstick? In fact, plenty of the ingredients of these brews were real drugs. A typical witches' brew might have contained deadly nightshade (belladonna), henbane (*Hyoscyamus niger*), monkshood (*Aconitum napellus*) and thorn-apple (*Datura stramonium*). All these plants contain potent narcotics and/or hallucinogenic substances which would certainly give you the feeling that you were flying or falling through space. The red toadstool with white spots, fly agaric, is also associated with witchcraft because it contains a hallucinogenic substances, muscarine. Even the toad was there for a chemical reason; the skin of the common toad contains another hallucinogenic poison, bufotenine. These witches' brews were commonly made into ointments and rubbed over the body, especially under the armpits. This procedure also had a sound scientific reason; the drugs would be absorbed through the skin, especially where the skin was soft, and you would be less likely to suffer from the acute poisoning and stomach upsets which would result from taking them by mouth.

Old lore about the time at which plants should be gathered

may also contain sound scientific advice. Even if you do not care to believe old alchemical notions about the virtues of dew collected from plants, certain plants are best picked in the early morning. The atropine content of belladonna and the morphine content of opium poppy juice can be four times greater in the morning than at other times of day. Plants, like animals, have hormones which ebb and flow according to a 'biological clock'. Dr William Withering, the English physician who first investigated the medicinal properties of the foxglove (see page 63), discovered that the foxglove leaves' were most potent when the flower was in bloom.

For many readers I suspect that old lore, witchcraft, the theory of the elements and humours and the Doctrine of Signatures are interesting simply as an exercise in nostalgia. We can patronisingly pat our ancestors on the back for the insights they occasionally gained and laugh up our sleeves at what seem to be fanciful mystical philosophies. Nevertheless, there are scientists who believe that we are neglecting and undervaluing the knowledge gained in the past and that we would do well to retrieve some of this ancient information before it – and the plants to which it refers – are lost for ever.

Useful plants

In the early 1960s a team of researchers at Harvard University led by Dr Siri von Reis Altschul thought it might be interesting to look through the university's archives. These archives contained no less than two-and-a-half million specimen sheets which had been left with the university by botanists during the preceding two centuries. The specimen sheets gave the name of the plant, its habitat and notes on the uses, if any, to which the plants had been put by local people. The team set out to find all the plants which were alleged to have some value as food or medicine. After four-and-a-half years they had identified 5,000 plants from this collection which they thought would be worth taking a closer look at.

In Britain we have two major plant collections, at Kew and in the British Museum, which contain three times as many specimens as the Harvard collection. The eight million specimens come from all over the world and have represented the botanical research of more than three hundred years. The specimen sheets are in many cases the only written record of the plant in question, because they were brought from places where the inhabitants did not write. Over the years many of these tribes have been wiped out or dispersed, taking their traditional knowledge with them: all that remains of their plant lore are the odd jottings of the itinerant botanists.

In 1980 pharmacist Dr Peter Hylands of Chelsea College, London, and Dr Malcolm Stuart, director of the Economic and Medicinal Plants Research Association (EMPRA) in Cambridge launched an appeal for funds to get these British collections investigated as the Harvard ones had been. Judging by the success of the Harvard study, Hylands and Stuart are confident that they should be able to identify 40,000 useful plants. They point out that the English collections are much bigger than the Harvard ones and that their study would not be confined to foods and medicines; if timbers, dyes and fibres were included the yield could be twice as large. They estimate that the project would cost about a million pounds, a tidy sum for running through the archives, but not so expensive if they were really able to identify 40,000 'new' useful plants.

Since 1960 the National Cancer Institute in the United States has been investigating plant extracts for potential anti-cancer properties. Out of the 100,000 extracts from the 29,000 plants they have looked at, around 3,000 showed some ability to fight animal tumours. Only a handful of these plant medicines have got to the stage of trials with human patients, but some look very promising.

A potent anti-cancer drug has been extracted from the may-apple, *Podophyllum peltatum*. It comes from North America, where Indian medicine men had long used it for treating tumours.

Although a handful of usable drugs might not seem to be much of a yield from 29,000 plants, this is the same kind of 'wastage' rate that pharmaceutical chemists expect to encounter when they are producing synthetic chemicals which might have medicinal use. The larger drug companies each turn out many thousands of new chemical formulations every year; less than one in a thousand ends up as a drug on the pharmacy shelf.

Despite the occasional interest shown by well-endowed organisations like the National Cancer Institute, the search for useful plants is still largely being conducted by enthusiastic individuals with few funds at their disposal. I quoted one such researcher at the beginning of this chapter. To get an idea of what scientists like him are doing and where they think their research might take them, let us adjourn to his laboratory at St Bartholomew's Hospital, London.

Dr Gorinsky in his laboratory

Dr Conrad Gorinsky, a tall dark man dressed – as a scientist should be – in a white lab coat, stands next to a glass chamber eight foot tall which contains a murky, grey-green ferment of leaves and stems. He looks like some twentieth-century Merlin, and does not object to being compared to a wizard.

'Chemists today serve exactly the same function as herbalists, alchemists and magicians did in the past,' he says. 'Our job, like theirs was, is to investigate and manipulate the substances of nature, to suggest explanations of the nature of life and to provide medicines, poisons and other compounds useful to our fellows.'

Nor is Dr Gorinsky afraid to communicate with people well outside the orthodox scientific circles to further his research. The unappetising-looking plant being examined in his laboratory is one of many he has collected from Indians living in the South American jungles of Brazil, Venezuela and Guyana, several of which have yielded potentially valuable drugs. One of them, cunaniol, comes from a plant which the Amazonians use as a poison to catch fish. It has the remarkable effect of 'stopping the heart dead in its tracks'. However, this effect is reversible: once the drug is washed out the heart will start up again. A drug like this could prove useful in open heart surgery. Warifteine, a substance which Dr Gorinsky has isolated from a shrub called *Cissampelos ovalifolia* which the Amazonians use in their curare arrow poisons, has shown itself to be a potent local anaesthetic and blood-pressure regulator. It is also used by the local women as a contraceptive, as is the greenheart tree, *Ocotea rodiaei*. Dr Gorinsky cites three other plants, all very different, each of which seems to cry out for further investigation:

Guayule, a plant which grows in desert conditions and produces a substance very similar to rubber;

Justicia petoralis, used by the Amazonians as a cough treatment and sedative; and

'Seje', a species of palm, whose nuts produce an oil very similar to olive oil.

Though Dr Gorinsky has facilities in his laboratories at St Bartholomew's Hospital for examining the basic chemical constituents of the plants he collects and for testing them on animals if necessary, the chances of their being taken up by an organisation or commercial enterprise with funds to do the full research which is needed before these substances could appear on the market seem slim. Pharmaceutical companies are generally unwilling to put up the millions of pounds needed to put a drug through the clinical trials demanded by law unless they are likely to get a return on their investment. They therefore tend to be more interested in synthetic chemicals, which they can patent, rather than plants, which are available to anyone who gathers them.

This is what recently happened when doctors in the United States realised that cannabis was a useful drug for cancer patients. A number of young patients with leukaemia admitted to their doctors that they smoked marijuana because it stopped them being sick when they took their cancer drugs. Cannabis seems to have been quite widely used by British doctors during the nineteenth century. Indeed, Dr J. Russell Reynolds, who was Physician in Ordinary to Queen Victoria and President of the Royal College of Physicians, declared in *The Lancet* that

> '*Indian hemp, when pure and administered carefully, is one of the most valuable medicines we possess*'.

He recommended it for insomnia, neuralgia, migraine, gout pains, convulsions, asthma and period pains. (It would be interesting to know whether he ever prescribed it to the Queen herself!) As recently as 1941 Professor A. D. McDonald of Manchester University wrote in the scientific journal *Nature* that 'in the clinical experience of many alienists [ie psychiatrists] a good preparation of hemp is incomparably the best drug for depressive mental conditions'. However, the fact that cannabis had been made an illegal drug later deterred doctors from prescribing it, until this new application in cancer therapy came to notice.

Nausea and vomiting are a distressing and gruesome side effect of the drugs used for treating leukaemia, and American cancer specialists were obviously interested in anything which might spare their patients such discomfort. So doctors at the Sidney Farber Institute in Boston and at the National Cancer Institute near Washington conducted a series of studies to see whether tetrahydro-cannabinol, the main chemical active in cannabis, was as effective as their young patients had suggested it might be. And they found that it was indeed a good anti-emetic for most patients. It also stimulated their patients' appetite and helped them sleep.

They were faced with two problems, however. Firstly, some patients enjoyed the psychic effect of the drug – the 'high' as it is more popularly known – but others did not; they got the horrors.

Cannabis leaves

Secondly, because cannabis was illegal, the doctors had to get their supplies from government sources, and there was no likelihood of the law being changed to allow doctors to prescribe it freely.

At this stage one of the big American drug companies entered the field, spending several millions of dollars on research to produce a synthetic, cannabis-like drug which would have the same anti-emetic effect but fewer of the psychic effects. Trials of the new drug that their chemists evolved are still in progress in the USA, West Germany and at the Christie Hospital in Manchester. The preliminary results suggest that this synthetic drug Levonantradol is as good as, perhaps better than, cannabis tincture as an anti-emetic, but that the effects on the mind are still potent. If, as seems likely, this drug does establish itself as useful for cancer patients and is passed by government drug-safety committees, then the drug company should be able to profit from its research. Nevertheless it will be a much more expensive drug than cannabis, which is an extremely easy plant to cultivate, and despite the clinical trials it will have been through, it will still be a brand new drug about which much less is known than we know about cannabis. In stating this it is not intended to disparage the clever research done by these chemists, but to illustrate how legal and financial considerations can prompt industry to seek complicated solutions to problems which could be quite easily solved with plant materials that are already to hand.

The moral climate is as prejudicial to cannabis today as it was to tomatoes in Victorian times. Quite a fuss was kicked up when these now familiar vegetables were first brought in to Britain from the Continent, for they were widely believed to be aphrodisiac, and had the nickname 'love apples'. (This idea is still reflected in the Italian word for tomato: *pomadoro*.)

Even cocoa, surely regarded by most people as one of the most innocuous of beverages, would probably have a hard time getting past our current food and drug laws. As Dr Gorinksy points out, 'cocoa contains theobromine and a variety of other stimulant alkaloids; it would be deemed unthinkable as a bedtime drink for young children!' Tea and coffee would probably fare no better, for they too, of course, contain stimulant drugs.

The idea of banning cocoa, tea and coffee seems ludicrous. They are part of our tradition, everyone is familiar with them, even if they do produce the odd mild side effect now and then. Nobody would turn round and condemn coffee as a dangerous drug just because your head can go into a bit of a spin after you've drunk six cups of it. Everyone knows from experience what the benefits and risks of these beverages are; and this general knowledge makes them acceptably safe.

'They have passed what I would call the ethnobiological test', comments Conrad Gorinsky. 'Ethnobiology' is a fancy term for the interaction of people with their natural environment, and Dr Gorinsky, in common with other scientists involved in plant medicine research, believes that an ethnobiological approach to drug research might provide us with more useful medicines than a synthetic chemist could dream of.

What the ethnobiological approach means in practical terms is that researchers would try to learn new ways of using plants from different cultures. If a plant had been used for generations by a people for a particular purpose without causing them any obvious deleterious effects, it would be studied more closely.

Herbalists have traditionally followed this approach, passing knowledge from generation to generation and testing it in their own everyday practice. The ethnobiological approach has also borne fruit in orthodox medicine. Rauwolfia, used in India for centuries as a mild sedative, was 'discovered' by Western medicine in the 1940s and widely prescribed as a tranquilliser and blood-pressure reducing agent ever since. The muscle-relaxant curare drugs were first discovered by the South American Indians, who had found that juices extracted from chondodendron and strychnos plants were a highly effective arrow poison which brought their prey to the ground quickly and silently. In 1923 the Madagascan periwinkle, *Vinca rosea*, enjoyed passing celebrity as a breakthrough for diabetes. Like its European cousin, *Vinca major*, this periwinkle had been used by African herbalists for treating diabetes. In the long run it turned out not to be as good a treatment as insulin, but once the research chemists had started investigating it in depth, this little plant yielded something just as valuable. It is now the source of two important drugs, vinblastine and vincristine, used for treating leukaemia.

Rather than search through old plant archives, Dr Gorinsky believes in visiting the people who still use plants as a matter of course and necessity. The Amazonian Indian peoples are one of the best sources of information, he suggests, because they live in a part of the humid tropics which contains over three quarters of the plant species of the world.

'The Amazonian tribes know every species which grows in their locality, and their knowledge is the reason for their continuing survival. They may not be able to read, they may not be able to understand the language of tribes living fifty miles away, but these people hold ninety per cent of mankind's current practical knowledge of plants. Unfortunately both these people and their plants are becoming endangered species as the Amazon basin is opened up by croppers and settlers.'

The medicinal plants used by native herbalists may have two great advantages over the synthetic chemicals which are being turned out in such great numbers by the drug companies. Firstly, very often they have chemical structures quite unlike anything previously seen. 'The chances against any laboratory chemist producing a molecule like that of cunaniol or warifteine are a million to one,' Dr Gorinsky comments. Secondly, the plants used by native herbalists have been tested on people for generations. So if a drug company or government agency wanted to investigate the contraceptive potential of warifteine or the greenheart tree, they would have a human population immediately at hand which had tested the plant on itself. In the normal course of events a new drug undergoes its first tests on rats or mice. Though these animals do have some basic similarities to humans, there are also of course some quite radical differences. So just as the hazards of a drug may not reveal themselves until it has been tried on humans for a long period, conversely the possible benefits of a drug for humans may not be revealed by tests on laboratory animals.

The ethnobiological approach has produced dividends in China where scientists have found that cottonseed oil is an effective male contraceptive. In parts of southern China and Tibet cottonseed oil is used in cooking, and it had not occurred to these people that it might have any effect on reproduction. But when researchers were trying to work out why the birth rate in certain communities was markedly lower than in other parts of the country, they wondered whether this unusual dietary substance might be the reason. It now emerges that a substance in cottonseed oil called gossypol can make men temporarily infertile by somehow interfering with the growth of sperm cells. The tests which have been carried out so far show that gossypol has no effect on libido, sexual inclination, and that the temporary infertility disappears after the man stops taking it.

India and Africa have another herb which is used by *hakims* and 'witch doctors' as a contraceptive for women. *Abrus precatorius* is a wild shrub which bears brightly coloured red and black seeds. Eaten whole these seeds are poisonous, but when the husk is peeled off, the soft inner part of the seed provides what is claimed to be a once-a-month contraceptive pill. Dr Mohammed Aslam, a Nottingham University pharmacist, who has been studying *hakims'* medicines in India and Britain (he found these *Abrus precatorius* seeds being sold by Asian herbalists in Bradford), points out that no proper long-term studies have been made of women who use this medicine, but that the available evidence from generations of use does indeed suggest that it does what it is claimed to do. Another interesting Asian herbal medicine has come to Dr Aslam's attention. Like gossypol, it is a male contraceptive, and it comes from a plant called *Andrographis paniculata*. This medicine has not been formally tested on humans either, but animal experiments have shown that it has a reversible effect like that of gossypol.

The fact that a herb has been used for generations does not necessarily mean that it is safe, however. East African herbalists have traditionally prescribed juice from a herb called crotalaria against measles; it was only recently that health workers realised that people who had taken much of this medicine were getting liver damage. In West Africa dried cow dung (which is herbal material of a kind) is still being used by untrained local midwives to dress the severed umbilical cord on newborn babies. In areas where many babies die shortly after birth, it had not occurred to them that the cow dung was causing tetanus and was a major cause of infant mortality.

Sometimes a herbal medicine presents a hazard simply because it is being used with other substances which interact with it or increase its effect. A herb called karella, *Momordica charantia*, which can be bought in Asian groceries in Britain because it is a popular flavouring for curry, is also used by *hakims* for treating diabetes. Karella reduces the amount of sugar circulating in the blood and is therefore a quite reasonable treatment for this disease. However, Dr Aslam came across a woman who had been taking this herb from her *hakim* as well as diabetes drugs from her NHS general practitioner. Her blood sugar had fallen so low that she had to be admitted to hospital in near coma.

Third World

Although western medicine has profited from medicinal plants first exploited by herbalists in Africa, Asia and South America and could doubtless gain many more drugs from herbs so far neglected, it is perhaps the Third World countries themselves which stand to gain most from healing herbs. On the subject of drugs for diabetes, for instance, Dr Robert Bannerman, former director of the World Health Organisation's education programme, pointed out to me that the West was already well provided with medicines which it could afford and which were freely available. 'But in an African village,' he commented, 'even if people can get hold of insulin they may not be able to get syringes for injecting it. And if they can get syringes they have problems keeping them sterile. In that context it makes a lot more sense for them to take an infusion of a local herb.'

In an interview with the medical journal *World Medicine* in 1979 Dr Oku Ampofo, director of the Centre for Scientific Research into Plant Medicine in Ghana, explained why his government was actively studying the work of traditional herbalists. Many Ghanaians needed medical treatment when they were many hundreds of miles from a modern hospital. If a farmer cut his arm with a machete, he could not do what a city dweller would do – rush to a casualty department, to have the wound stitched and dressed and get a shot of tetanus serum.

> *'The people in the bush have plants which stop even arterial bleeding. You wash the leaves, chew them, put them on the wound and cover them with a bandage. The leaves have both antibiotic and coagulant effects on the wound, and you get clean healing in three days.'*

Dr Ampofo and his investigators do not just take traditional herbs to their laboratories to see what effect isolated extracts of the plants may have on cultures in test tubes. They believe that it is better to look at the herbal preparations which are formulated by the traditional herbalists themselves. Like many British herbalists, who argue that medicines made from whole plants are safer and possibly even more effective than the individual chemical ingredients which pharmacists like to isolate from medicinal herbs, Dr Ampofo holds that the whole plant may contain a host of useful substances.

> *'The western world does not yet know how fully to analyse a plant. There are certain enzymes we cannot isolate, but which we know do useful work.'*

Western technical expertise in pharmacognosy (the study of medicinal plants) and traditional African herbal knowledge have recently been brought together in Rome, where the Istituto Italo-Africano has embarked on a project sponsored by the World Health Organisation. The project is twofold: to test the claims made for traditional herbs trying to find out whether they have unsuspected side effects and to draw up a list of plants which can be cultivated in different parts of the world to cover basic medical needs.

The aim is to give Third World countries the means to become less dependent on 'developed' nations for their drugs, because, by Third World standards, western drugs are very expensive.

Herbal medicine in Britain

Herbal medicine is not just a Third World phenomenon, though. Professional herbalists in Britain may still be outnumbered two hundred to one by general practitioners, but they continue to thrive. The laws which govern the practice of medicine in this country are relatively liberal, and anyone can sell fresh powdered or dried herbs for medical purposes.

Herbal medicine is controlled by rather more regulations than other forms of alternative medicine, however. When the Medicines Act was introduced in 1968, restrictions were placed on a number of the more potentially poisonous herbs. So although there is no law to prevent you from trying to grow foxglove, mistletoe, nux vomica, poison ivy or rauwolfia in your garden for your own use, the Medicines Act forbids you to sell or prescribe them to anyone else – unless you are a qualified doctor or pharmacist. Other herbs which herbalists are not allowed to supply are: areca, Canadian hemp, *Catha edulis*, *Chenopodium ambrosiodes*, *Cocculus indicus*, *Crotalaria*, croton oil, croton seed, *Cucurbita maxima*, *Duboisia*, *Elaterium*, *Embelia*, ergot, *Erysimum canescens*, *Holarrhena*, ignatius bean, kamala, kousso, male fern, *Podophyllum*, pomegranate bark,

Sabadilla, santonica, savin, *Scopolia*, stavesacre seeds, *Stropanthus*, slippery elm bark, *Veratrum* and yohimbe bark.

There is another group of herbs which can be supplied by herbalists but only within limited dosages and with these dosages and the name of the remedy clearly written on the container. These include aconite, adonis, belladonna, celandine, cinchona, colchicum, conium, convallaria, ephedra, gelsemium, henbane, jaborandi, lobelia, poison oak, quebracho, ragwort and thorn-apple.

Despite these restrictions, herbalists still have more than 300 herbs which they can use freely in their practices. In the next chapter a herbalist and a doctor comment on the effectiveness of many of the more widely recommended herbal medicines, drawn from a variety of standard 'herbal' books.

How herbal medicines are made

For cooking, herbs are best used fresh and raw, but medical herbalists usually find it impossible to keep large stocks of fresh herbs on hand. Moreover a leaf, flower, stem or root, especially if it is dried, is often not very palatable. So most herbal medicines are preparations which are designed to keep well and to be administered easily.

Herbal preparations can be taken internally as pills or liquid medicines or externally as lotions, foot baths, compresses, enemas and so on.

Any readers thinking of making herbal remedies for themselves should beware, however. The chemical potency of herbs can vary greatly and without specialist knowledge and resources it is very difficult to ascertain the strength of a home-brewed remedy. While no one is likely to do themselves much harm with an infusion of a mild herb like thyme or chamomile, the preparation of medicines from strong herbs such as valerian is best left to the professional. **This book is not a manual for making your own medicines.**

Infusions are probably the simplest preparations. Basically, they are made in the same way as you make a pot of tea. You put the herb, or whichever part of the herb you want to infuse, into a pot and pour boiling water over it, allowing it to brew for about five minutes. You then strain it and drink the infusion. Herbs with very soft leaves may not have to be brewed for so long, although others with tough, fibrous leaves may need longer.

One of the problems with infusion is that if the plant contains volatile oils (like the thymol in thyme), these may evaporate from an ordinary teapot. One way herbalists prevent these volatile oils from escaping is to make the infusion inside a large vacuum flask (with the top screwed on, of course). The herbs are placed into a little metal basket or on a removable mesh hung inside the flask near the top and above the boiling water. In this way the oils are drawn out by the steam, and the plant material can be withdrawn without sullying the liquid.

Decoctions are made from the tougher parts of the plant like the stalks, seeds, bark or roots. The herb is put into a cold or lukewarm water, heated up slowly and allowed to boil for several minutes.

Juices are obviously extracted from only fresh herbs. A juicing machine can be used, which separates the juice from the pips and pith, or the plant can be crushed with a rolling pin or mortar and pestle. Sometimes the easiest way of applying the juice is simply to press the leaves or stem, squeezing the juice out directly on the skin.

Macerations are called for when the essential ingredients of the herb might be adversely affected by heat or if they take a long time to leach out. The herb is steeped in alcohol – white wine, spirits, cider or beer – and left for several days. Herbs should not be macerated in water alone because they would become contaminated with bacteria within hours. Alcohol is found to be an excellent preservative, so macerations will keep longer than infusions and decoctions, which really need to be refrigerated and consumed within a day or two.

Tinctures are more potent in every way. Here the herb is crushed and steeped in strong alcohol (70° proof or stronger), left for three days, then the liquid is strained and re-bottled. The alcohol is effective at drawing out the essential oils, and the solution – quite apart from its alcoholic strength – will be much stronger than a maceration. Tinctures may keep for a month or longer, but they do tend to weaken with time.

Poultices are an external application. The whole leaf of the plant is 'bruised' (slightly crushed) and applied directly to the lesion. They can be held in place with a cotton-wool pad or piece of gauze bandage. Alternatively a dried, powdered herb is sprinkled on the wound and kept in place in the same way.

Hot poultices can be made by boiling up a strong infusion or decoction (approximately two tablespoonfuls of herb to half a pint of water) and soaking the gauze in the liquid, allowing the excess liquid to drain off before applying the poultice to the skin. The poultice should not itself be boiling hot; 50°C is found to be warm enough. Regular removing and replacing of the poultice keep the lesion clean and maintain the herb's healing and relieving power.

Herbal oils can be prepared by steeping bruised herbs in a vegetable oil (like olive oil) in a warm, sunny place for a couple of weeks. Herbal oils are used as skin applications when a poultice is found to be too cumbersome. However, they should not be confused with essential oils, which are the actual volatile oils of the herb itself. Extracting essential oils is a complicated job, best left to the professional. **Essential oils should not be taken internally.**

Lotions, on the other hand, are simply strong infusions or decoctions which are rubbed or massaged into the skin. Lotions are found to be ideal for minor skin ailments and for the hair.

Herbs in Practice

Anyone who has taken the least interest in herbs will know that
almost every publisher seems to have at least one herbal on his list.
As well as being vast, this herbal literature is confusing and sometimes contradictory. Many writers, it would appear, have simply
plundered other works for their material and apparently repeated
what they found without comment, criticism or further enquiry.
Some books seem unable to distinguish one kind of complaint from
another, and appear to assume that if a herb can be used to treat one
kind of chest disease, for example, it can be used to treat them all.

There is no scope in a small book like this to go into minute
detail about the properties of all herbs, or even of the few hundred
commonly used by professional herbalists. I have taken a sample of
the remedies offered by a variety of herb books and asked two experts
to comment on them. The experts were Dr William A. R. Thomson,
former editor of *The Practitioner*, compiler of *Black's Medical Diction-
ary* and author of *Herbs That Heal*, and Simon Mills, a physiologist
by training and herbalist by profession who is Research Director of
the National Institute of Medical Herbalists. Neither expert would
claim to know all there is to know about this vast and ancient
subject, but both are qualified to comment scientifically and from
experience.

Aphrodisiacs

Aphrodisiacs (medicines which arouse sexual desire) are a prime example of the way in which herbalism can sometimes rely more on myth and suggestion than on any real physical effect of the plants. We can say without fear of contradiction that there is no plant which has chemical properties that will induce someone who has no desire for you to fall willingly into your arms. Herbalists and their clients have tried just about everything for possible aphrodisiac properties. One popular herbal lists no less than fifty-four substances which have been claimed to be aphrodisiac, and names cannabis, damiana, ergot, fo-ti-tieng, ginseng, jasmine, saw palmetto, stramonium and strychnine (nux vomica) as 'particularly efficacious'. Another book by a French author, under treatments for impotence, names garlic, aniseed, basil, hogweed, celandine, cabbage, fenugreek, lavender, mint, rosemary, savory and sage, and claims that the best is a clove of garlic rubbed on the base of the spine! If any of these herbs are really good aphrodisiacs, how come none of them appears in both of the authors' lists?

One herb which was mentioned in a number of books was male fern. Despite the sexual connotations of its name, Dr Thomson commented that the only proven medicinal use for male fern was as a cure for tapeworm. Obviously anyone who has a tapeworm might lose much of his or her normal vigour, which would return once the worm had been eliminated. But it would be rather far-fetched to claim that the herb was an aphrodisiac *per se*.

Our experts agreed that suggestion was the most potent aphrodisiac. If the patient was assured, and believed, that the medicine presented by the herbalist would stir the loins, then it very likely would, unless the patient had some genuine physical malfunction. Nevertheless some of the herbs named above do contain potent drugs. Strychnine, for example, is a general stimulant of the nervous system. Damiana leaf, Simon Mills pointed out, though much milder than strychnine, was more widely used by herbalists as a 'nerve tonic'.

Saw palmetto contains a hormone rather like oestrogen, and its fruit is used for treating prostate problems which affect elderly men; 'But to suggest that it was aphrodisiac would be a bit strong,' Mills commented.

Ginseng contains, among many other things, saponins, which

can mimic the effect of the female sex hormones like oestrogen. Finnish doctors have found that taking ginseng improves the production of mucus in the membranes of the sexual organs of women undergoing the menopause. It is, of course, also much praised for its general stimulating 'tonic' effects.

The best of the bunch of so-called aphrodisiacs, might be cannabis, Mills thought. Cannabis has been used through the ages for intensifying all sexual experiences, and, like alcohol, for lifting inhibitions. But it is, of course, illegal to grow, possess or sell it.

Hops, the brewer's herb, have a reputation as an aphrodisiac which may not be far-fetched. They contain oestrogenic substances which are chemically similar to the female sex hormones. However, although oestrogens may gently stimulate the female sexual cycle and add a youthful glow to the complexion at the same time, they are likely to have an anti-aphrodisiac effect on men. Indeed, hops are also used by herbalists as a tranquilliser and cure for insomnia, so they may just make our would-be lovers fall asleep.

Asthma, bronchitis, coughs and throat infections

Judging by the remedies they give for asthma and bronchitis, it would appear that some authors of herb books believe asthma and bronchitis to be the same thing and curable by the same remedies. Yet they are in fact different: asthma is the result of a spasm of the muscles which control the opening and closing of the airways of the lungs, whereas bronchitis is an inflammation of the airways, usually accompanied by congestion. It is of course possible to suffer from both at the same time, and some of the remedies for asthma may be effective in congestive bronchitis too.

Coltsfoot is listed indiscriminately in many books as a treatment for asthma, bronchitis and coughs. It can be taken as an infusion, or decoction or its dried leaves can be smoked in a pipe or cigarettes. Coltsfoot's main virtue is that it relieves muscle spasm in the airways. It is therefore useful for relieving asthma and suppressing coughs, but would be of less use if you needed an expectorant to bring up the phlegm from your lungs.

Elecampane

Horehound, hyssop and elecampane, on the other hand, which appear regularly under the heading of asthma treatments, are more effective as expectorants. With horehound and hyssop the leaves and flowers are made into an infusion; in the case of elecampane it is the roots which are infused.

Other herbs commonly listed as asthma treatments include marsh mallow, marjoram and ephedra. All parts of the marsh mallow have a soothing effect on mucous membranes and on airways when an infusion is taken internally. Marjoram contains a volatile oil which can relax the smooth muscle of the airways, though Simon Mills was sceptical about the infusions of marjoram prescribed in some books. In an ordinary infusion, he pointed out, the volatile oil would simply evaporate from the hot liquid and disappear. If the patient wanted to extract the maximum effect from the small amount of volatile oil available in the plant, it would be best to infuse the herb inside a thermos flask so that the precious oil could not escape.

Ephedra, a Chinese herb, contains ephedrine, which is also used in orthodox medicine as a drug which acts on the sympathetic nervous system, stimulating the so-called 'fight or flight' mechanism and opening the airways. Known in Chinese as Ma-huang, ephedra is an ingredient of several prescriptions listed in *The Barefoot Doctor's Manual*, along with − believe it or not − toasted grasshoppers, pulverised earthworms and goat's bile. Our experts knew little of the virtues of these last named remedies, but were in no doubt about the efficacy of ephedra. They pointed out, however, that it would only relieve symptoms; it could not prevent an attack from occurring.

An asthma remedy which appears in very few books but which is highly prized by herbalists is stramonium otherwise known as datura or thorn-apple. In large amounts stramonium is a hallucinogenic drug − witches used to take it to give themselves the illusion that they were flying − and although it can be prescribed by a herbalist, the herb itself is no longer allowed to be sold directly over the counter to the public. Both our experts considered that it could be helpful, smoked like a cigarette, but pointed out that it would be a dangerous drug in inexperienced hands.

Among other herbal remedies often mentioned for bronchitis (apart from elecampane, hyssop and horehound) are mullein, sage and lungwort. Lungwort's very name suggests that it might be an old remedy for bronchitis, though according to some herbal historians the name is due more to its colour and shape (it has egg-

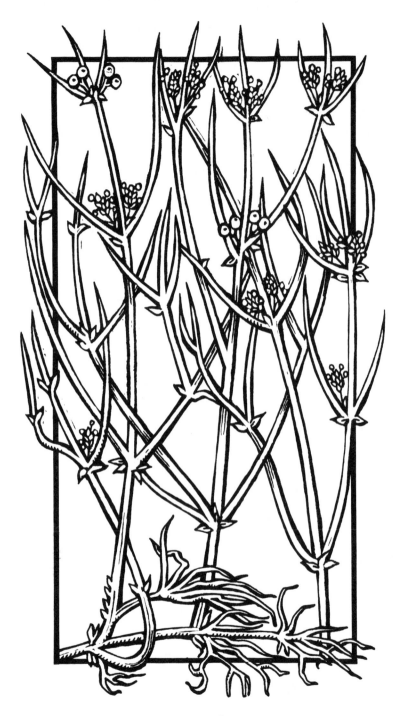

Ephedra

shaped leaves with white spots which, to some eyes, make it look like lungs). So its alleged virtues in this field may owe something to the old Doctrine of Signatures, though the plant does contain a mucilage which would be soothing for grastro-intestinal and bronchial tissue. Mullein is also rich in soothing mucilage and contains saponins which, Simon Mills suggests, would make it a good expectorant. Sage contains antiseptic volatile oils which Simon Mills thought might make it useful for treating infections of the upper respiratory tract (coughs and colds) if it was gargled. 'Sage also has the property of reducing secretions such as salivation and lactation, so it might help dry up catarrh,' he speculated.

Other plant remedies for throat infections are lemon and eucalyptus. Both experts agreed that the vitamin C in lemon was valuable, if not vital, for anyone stricken with an infection. Mills declared that the fruit acids and flavenoids of lemon, not just the vitamin C alone, were important. Eucalyptus, Dr Thomson pointed out, was mildly antiseptic as well as being a decongestant. 'Put a drop of eucalyptus oil on your pillow before you go to sleep. It will help you breathe more easily if you have a cold or sore throat.'

Gastro-intestinal ailments

including stomach ulcers, constipation, diarrhoea and herbs which prevent griping and aid digestion

When talking about herbs for the stomach and gut, we should distinguish between those which merely soothe and those which may have some healing power against serious troubles. Anyone who has a stomach ulcer will be spared from some of their suffering if they can reduce the amount of acid in their stomach. But relief from symptoms is not the same as a cure, for which more potent medicines may be required.

A whole host of herbs are recommended by various authors as digestives and carminatives. Digestives are supposed to aid digestion, while carminatives relieve griping pains and help get rid of excess 'wind'.

'All the common culinary herbs like rosemary, sage and thyme are both digestives and carminatives,' says Simon Mills. But the most potent digestives, he suggests, are the bitters, which include gentian, wormwood, barberry and dandelion root. (Barberry, *Berberis vulgaris*, should not be confused with bearberry, *Uva ursi*, which is also used in herbal medicine as a urinary antiseptic for conditions like cystitis.) Bitters, he explains, 'switch on' the digestive tract, encouraging the formation of gastric juices and prompting the liver to produce bile. It is their bitter taste which sets these things in action, so there is probably little point in taking some herbal digestives sold in the shops which contain other ingredients to mask the bitter taste. Vermouth and coffee are popular digestives which work on this bitter principle. Vermouth is wine with an added maceration of bitter herbs: the word is a corruption of 'wormwood'. Alcohol itself, Dr Thomson explained, was a digestive too in moderate amounts; it helps by dilating the blood vessels around the stomach. Alcohol, coffee and bitters are not likely to be of any use to someone suffering from an ulcer, however. They would only serve to irritate it further.

For griping pains chamomile flowers, taken as a tea, are widely recommended for their relaxant properties, and Simon Mills suggested that hops and lemon balm infusions, also used for treating 'nerves', were useful in this context. The aromatic herbs lavender, fennel, dill and aniseed were useful for relieving chronic wind, he added. Infusions of lavender flowers or the seeds of the other three are the standard domestic remedies.

Anyone suffering from stomach ulcers might think twice before opting for herbal medicine rather than more orthodox treatment, but it is quite likely that whether he went to a herbalist or a Harley Street doctor he might well end up with basically the same prescription. For liquorice is not only a herbal remedy used throughout the world for gastric ulcers; it is also the basis of a commonly prescribed orthodox medicine. In his book *Herbs That Heal*, Dr Thomson tells the story of how a Dutch doctor during the Second World War revived his profession's lost interest in liquorice. This doctor, F.E.Revers, noticed that some of his patients with stomach ulcers were doing particularly well and found out that they were all taking a medicine brewed up for them by the local chemist which contained large amounts of liquorice extract. Liquorice has an effect like cortisone and a real ability to promote the healing of gastric ulcers. It does in large doses have side effects, however, notably high blood pressure and water retention. Some patients taking liquorice root preparations, whether herbal or those manufactured by pharmaceutical companies, get diarrhoea from it, though this is seldom severe. Liquorice is also an effective purgative; so it seems rather confusing that several of the better herb books should recommend liquorice infusions as a cure for diarrhoea!

Another widely recommended herbal remedy for stomach ulcers is comfrey, whose healing properties are described in the section on wounds (see page 55). Even when taken as an infusion it is rich in mucilage, which would have a soothing and unbinding effect on the gut.

Simon Mills recommended meadow-sweet which, like willow bark, is a rich source of salicylates with their aspirin-like pain-killing properties. Aspirin itself would be the last thing that most doctors would give to a patient with stomach ulcers, because one of the main problems with this drug is that it erodes the stomach lining and would aggravate an ulcer. However, Mills pointed out that meadow-sweet was also rich in mucilages which protect the stomach lining while allowing the active ingredient to have its anti-inflammatory effect. 'It is a natural version of the "buffered" brands of aspirin produced by the proprietary medicine manufacturers,' Mills commented.

For diarrhoea it is surprising to see many herbals recommend a variety of fruits, notably strawberry, bilberry, rose hips and raspberry. Fruits are more usually associated with causing 'the runs' than with curing them, but the value of most of these plants in the treatment of diarrhoea lies less in their fruit than in their leaves which, because they are rich in tannins, have a binding effect on the gut. Simon Mills suggested that a much richer source of tannins was the root of tormentil, *Potentilla erecta*. Various species of *Potentilla* are cultivated as garden shrubs.

For constipation oatmeal, senna, rhubarb and prune are recommended universally. Oatmeal is rich in fibrous bran which draws water into the digestive tract and makes stools bulky and free-moving. Prunes too are rich in edible fibre. Rhubarb and senna (both the leaves and the pods) are purgatives. Purgatives might be of use if you do not usually suffer from constipation, but it is undesirable to use them too often without trying to ascertain why you had constipation in the first place. If your constipation is due to a lack of dietary fibre, you would be much better advised to increase your fibre intake by eating wholemeal bread, fresh vegetables and fruit or raw bran with cereals, soups or drinks. If your constipation is due to 'nerves' or stress – a lot of people get constipated when they travel or are worried about something – you would treat your system more sympathetically by using a relaxant therapy rather than a purgative.

Anything which helps you relax will be useful for what could be called nervous constipation; warm baths, a walk in the country, a massage or perhaps a day off work would likely to be just as valuable as a herbal relaxant like chamomile, hops, crampbark and valerian (note that the last two are rather more drastic remedies than the first two). A French herbalist recommends that constipation should be treated with artichoke leaves, chamomile flowers, chicory leaves, cabbage leaves, mallow flowers, grated onion, thyme and violet. You are not supposed to drink these things but to steep them in foot baths and hand baths which are taken twice a day! Dr Thomson was sceptical about the value of foot baths and hand baths for treating an internal complaint like constipation, though Simon Mills was more enthusiastic, pointing out that there were fewer nicer ways to relax than with your feet in a steaming, sweet scented tub!

Hair tonics

The cure for baldness is sought with as much enthusiasm as the love philtre which will make beautiful ladies fall in love with donkeys. But there is no herbal cure for baldness – and hair transplants are beyond the scope of this book. Dandruff and falling hair maybe reversible, however, and the herbs which seem to be mentioned time and again are rosemary and stinging nettle.

Although our experts were sceptical about most of the proprietary 'herbal' shampoos on the market, as it is unclear how much herbal matter they contain, they were – rather to my surprise – both prepared to admit there might be something to be said for rosemary and stinging nettles. Simon Mills said that he saved his own scalp by adding a couple of drops of rosemary oil to the final rinse after washing the hair. This gives 'a delightful tingling sensation'. Dr Thomson suggested that nettle preparations could get rid of scurf and dandruff by stimulating the blood flow in the scalp, which would in turn improve the health of the hair.

Rosemary is said to add colour to greying hair. Dr Thomson thought it more likely that the herb, rather than dying the hair, helped to get rid of unhealthy hair which had lost its original colour.

Various recipes are recommended for both herbs in this context: infusions and oil extracts for rosemary and infusions and macerations for nettle. This is rather surprising in the case of nettle, because very hot water will destroy some of the ingredients like formic acid which stimulate the scalp; this is less likely to happen in maceration. However, as always, different preparations may suit different individuals.

Headaches, fevers, arthritis and rheumatism

This is a strange assortment of complaints to lump together under the same heading, you may think. There is, however, a noticeable overlap between these complaints and the herbal remedies used to relieve them. Feverfew, for example, occurs as a treatment for migraine, fever and arthritic pain. Willow bark similarly has a long history as a treatment for 'the ague', a malaria-like condition once common in Europe, the symptoms of which included fever, aches and pains. In orthodox medicine there is one drug which is used to treat all these conditions: the old familiar aspirin. One of the reasons aspirin is effective is that it checks the production of prostaglandins. Prostaglandins are involved in a variety of important bodily functions, but notably in pain and inflammation.

Herb books offer a bewildering variety of suggestions for relieving all these complaints. As well as the two herbs mentioned above, fennel, marjoram and rosemary were suggested for headaches; birch water (a sugary sap extracted by boring a small hole in the bark of the tree) and borage are among those suggested for fever; and for arthritis and rheumatism we are told of the virtues of mint, celery and stinging nettles.

As headache cures, our experts thought little of fennel, rosemary and marjoram, though they were more impressed by the claims made for feverfew. Feverfew has become a popular do-it-yourself treatment for migraine, though like all treatments for migraine, it works well for some people and not at all for others. Doubtless one of the main reasons why feverfew does work is that it contains an aspirin-like substance which checks production of prostaglandins.

Feverfew

However, as migraine sufferers will know, migraine headaches are brought on by different causes in different individuals. Some get their headache at times of stress, others after eating certain foods, and others for no apparent reason at all. Warning that feverfew was as bad for some people's migraines as it was good for others, Simon Mills offered a rule-of-thumb guide to its use. Some sufferers can get relief from their migraine by applying something hot to their heads, while others get relief from cold things like ice packs. 'If you are one of those who are helped by a heat, then feverfew is for you,' he suggested. 'Feverfew, like a hot application, dilates the blood vessels, whereas cold makes them contract. If your migraine is relieved by a cold pack, avoid feverfew.'

As for fever, neither expert had much to say for birch water. Birch water is basically sugar and can make a sweet, fizzy wine, so it might help restore energy. Borage is salty and might help replace salts lost from sweating.

Feverfew and willow bark undeniably have the ability to bring down fever. Willow bark, like feverfew, has its own aspirin-like substance; indeed, it is the original source of salicylic acid, the natural chemical which was used before chemists made modern synthetic aspirin (which is known chemically as acetyl salicylic acid). Salicylic acid occurs in many plants: meadow-sweet, *Spiraea ulmaria*, is one widely used by herbalists to bring down fever and is said to be gentler on the stomach than aspirin.

However, both Mills and Thomson warned that bringing down the temperature by artificial means was not really the best way to deal with fevers. The high temperature, they pointed out, was nature's way of reacting to an infection and that it might not be desirable to suppress this natural mechanism. An alternative to aspirin and its herbal equivalents would be preparations which actually encourage you to sweat. Simon Mills suggested hot infusions of yarrow, elderflowers, ginger, catmint or chamomile all of which can increase sweating but, paradoxically, cool you down soon afterwards.

Turning to arthritis and rheumatism, Simon Mills suggested that birch leaves, though not much use in fever, might be helpful here. Preparations of birch leaves, celery seed and dandelion root are all used by British herbalists as part of their treatment for arthritis. They are all diuretics, and the rationale is that they help 'cleanse' the body of accumulated wastes. Celery seed has been reported to reduce the level of uric acid circulating in the bloodstream; and if this is so, it would make it useful for treating gout which is caused by excess uric acid in the blood. Backache may be due to kidney problems rather than anything in the spine itself.

Heat is effective at temporarily easing joint pains. Mustard baths and mustard plasters are an effective heat treatment, Simon Mills suggested. Dr Thomson suggested that stinging nettles were effective for two reasons. They improved circulation in the affected area, and they were also a counter-irritant. Acupuncture and electrical stimulation of the skin are other examples of counter-irritants used for pain relief.

It seems that counter-irritants may work by stimulating different nervous pathways from those which are causing the underlying pain. Intense stimulation of these pathways causes the signals from other sources to be blotted out.

Insomnia, 'nerves' and stress

In medical parlance a 'sedative' is a drug which puts you to sleep or at least makes you drowsy. Several of the herbs which are listed as 'sedatives' in herb books are no more than tranquillisers.

'Opium is the best known and oldest herbal sedative,' Simon Mills pointed out, 'though herbalists in this country are of course no longer allowed to prescribe it.'

Probably the most potent herb that herbalists may prescribe is valerian, which Mills described as 'the herbalist's equivalent of valium'. Until about thirty years ago valerian was still widely prescribed by doctors for insomnia and for calming anxious and/or neurotic patients. The root is used in macerations or infusions. The resulting medicine tastes quite vile, but it is loved by cats. As well as having a proven depressive effect on the central nervous system, valerian also has the ability to regulate irregular heart rhythms and control convulsions. One herbal book suggests that mint, chamomile flowers and lavender flowers can be added to a valerian-root infusion; this would help disguise its taste.

Chamomile regularly appears as a treatment for insomnia and nerves. Simon Mills suggested that it was the ideal remedy for nervous children, not as strong as and far better-tasting than valerian. It is also a gentle digestive, and Dr Thomson reported that it is very popular as a nightcap in Italy.

Among other remedies named for insomnia we find hops and wild lettuce. Both experts agreed that hops was a very mild sedative, and that for insomnia the most effective way to use it was as a stuffing in pillows.

Passionflower and peach flower infusions appear in some books as 'sedatives'. Neither Mills nor Thomson had heard anything about the medicinal properties of peach flowers and commented that passionflower, better known perhaps by its scientific name *Passiflora*, was a mild relaxant.

Among the herbs recommended by various authors for 'nerves' are angelica, lemon balm and skullcap. The inclusion of angelica surprised our experts, who pointed out that it was used primarily as an expectorant. Balm, as its name suggests, is an old remedy for soothing frayed nerves, though herbalists now use it primarily as a digestive and as a treatment for mild fevers: it is another of those herbs which cool you down by making you sweat. Skullcap used to be in the pharmacopoeias as a remedy for headaches, neuralgia, convulsions and hysteria; it certainly seems to be a potent herb, because overdosage was reported to cause convulsions. Simon Mills from his own experience recommended crampbark, otherwise known as guelder rose, which also used to be in both American and British medical formularies as a treatment for nervous complaints, especially those which involved some kind of muscle spasm.

'Liver' and 'kidney' problems

The French have a disease which they call *crise de foie*, literally 'liver crisis', which has no real counterpart in British diagnostics. Anyone suffering from *une crise de foie* is regarded as being ill enough to merit time off work, and French doctors prescribe a variety of medicines to deal with this national scourge. It seems that the commonest reason for this complaint is over-indulgence in food and drink, so perhaps the closest English term for *crise de foie* would be 'hangover'.

'Most of the herbal remedies for these so-called liver disorders are purgatives which clear out the gut rather than act primarily on the liver,' Dr Thomson pointed out. However, some of the liver remedies do stimulate the production of bile, a fluid produced by the liver to get rid of waste products and to facilitate the digestion of fat in the digestive tract. Agrimony infusions and decoctions are recommended by various authors, though Simon Mills said that he would go for more bitter herbs like dandelion and wormwood. 'All bitters are good for hangovers,' he suggested.

Dandelion is also a potent diuretic. Diuretics are medicines which make you pass water, and they are needed in the treatment of heart failure, high blood pressure and other conditions where fluid is retained in the body. Diuretics encourage the kidneys to get rid of accumulated salts which are responsible for water retention. Dandelion's diuretic properties are celebrated in its nicknames 'Wet-the-bed' and in French, '*Pissenlit*'. The leaves can be eaten raw in a salad, or the root can be infused, made into a decoction, or dried and ground and used as dandelion 'coffee'. All parts of the plant have the diuretic effect. Dandelion may also have an advantage over the diuretic drugs like the thiazides which are used in conventional medicine. These drugs have to be given in conjunction with a potassium supplement because they make the body lose potassium along with fluid. Dandelion, on the other hand, is rich in potassium and can be given as a diuretic and potassium supplement in one.

One of the most famous herbal medicines, digitalis, the fox-glove, is a diuretic. Digitalis was originally prescribed for treating dropsy, the kind of water retention which results from heart failure. Digitalis does not act on the kidneys; it cures water retention by strengthening and regularising the contractions of the heart muscle, and once the heart is functioning properly, the improved blood circulation flushes the excess fluid out through the kidneys. However, digitalis can be dangerous in high doses and it tends to accumulate in the body. Herbalists, unless they are also qualified doctors or pharmacists, are no longer allowed to dispense it.

Parsley is also a good mild diuretic, the roots and/or seeds can be infused, though herbalists also extract the essential oils for putting into pills. Simon Mills commented that several herbs which appear in the handbooks under the heading of 'diuretics' or 'cures for kidney ailments' are really antiseptics which act in the urinary system and are therefore useful for relieving cystitis and urethritis. They include celery seed, horsetail, juniper berries and bearberry, all of which can be infused. Parsley too is useful against cystitis.

Although various herbs are recommended by herbals for treating kidney stones, bladder stones and gall stones, there is no evidence that any can actually cause stones to dissolve, though they may ease the pain somewhat. Plantain got a name as a cure for stones, but this was largely due to the principles of sympathetic magic of the Doctrine of Signatures. Plantain grows in stony ground and sometimes appears to have pushed its way through the rock.

Period problems

Again we find that a whole range of quite separate complaints tend to be coyly classified under the single heading of 'menstrual or period problems', and that some authors do not specify whether the remedies they recommend are for treating period pain, for excessive bleeding or for bringing the period on.

Herbalists have a word – emmenagogue – to describe any herb which brings periods on. Both our experts pointed out that this was often a thinly veiled euphemism for 'abortifacient'. One of the main reasons, before the introduction of the Abortion Act, why a woman might consult a herbalist rather than her family doctor was that she feared she was pregnant and did not want to have the child. She would therefore ask for something to bring her period on, and the herbalist, happy to keep up euphemistic appearances, would prescribe an 'emmenagogue'.

In fact herbalists were wise, apart from obvious legal reasons, not to claim that their herbs could procure abortions, because abortifacient herbs are as rare as the fabled love philtres. 'It is very difficult to induce an abortion in a healthy woman,' Dr Thomson commented. Many of the herbs recommended as emmenagogues or abortifacients principally affect the stomach and digestive tract, which though in very roughly the same geographical area of the body are not quite the same thing as the womb. Some, like the bitter wormwood, were probably taken on the principle that anything which tastes vile would be likely to provoke abortion. Yarrow and chamomile might be useful for period pains as they have relaxant properties.

Simon Mills said that professional herbalists would probably be more likely to use motherwort or shepherd's purse for dealing with period pain or heavy menstrual bleeding.

Skin afflictions

including cuts, boils, eczema, inflammation, corns and warts

The two most commonly named antiseptics for the skin, recommended for cleaning cuts and grazes, were thyme and garlic. These herbs can be prepared in various ways. Thyme leaves can be made into an infusion, which is used to wash the skin. Thymol, the essential oil, can also be applied directly to the skin or added to bath water. Garlic pulped with a mortar and pestle can be laid on the skin under a bandage, or garlic vinegar can be used as a skin wash.

Thymol has proven antiseptic properties, but Simon Mills did not think that an infusion of thyme would contain a strong enough solution of the oil to have much effect.

Crushed garlic may have helped to save soldiers' lives during the First World War. Soldiers in the trenches deprived of more conventional medicines used to dress wounds with garlic and sphagnum moss.

Garlic's botanical cousin, the onion, often cropped up as a treatment for boils. Most authors suggest that it should be either baked or boiled and applied directly.

Both garlic and onion do contain substances which kill certain bacteria and fungi, though garlic is the more potent of the two, because its essential oils are more concentrated and less volatile than those of the onion.

Thyme, garlic and onion have the advantage for the home herbalist of being freely available and found in almost every kitchen. But for the professional herbalist the most popular antiseptic is Echinacea, the purple coneflower.

'Echinacea is the herbalist's penicillin,' says Simon Mills. 'It is an American plant, and though not a great deal of research has been made into it, it is known to contain volatile oils with proven anti-staphylococcal properties and fungicidal resins.' It also contains phenolic acid, which kills bacteria, and a substance which acts against hyaluronidase, an enzyme which breaks down soft tissue.

Echinacea is usually taken internally. The root is ground to powder and taken in capsules or tablets. Dried roots can be bought in Britain but some authorities say that the dried root is nothing like as effective as fresh root. In this case the fluid extract may be better.

The purple coneflower, Echinacea

Marsh mallow is mentioned in dozens of herb books as a treatment for boils, abscesses and inflammation, but apart from agreeing that a marsh mallow poultice might have a soothing effect on inflamed skin, Thomson and Mills did not think much of it as a dressing for infected wounds.

As far as the more chronic skin conditions, like eczema, are concerned, few herb books offer much specific advice. Figwort is mentioned by one or two, though Simon Mills pointed out that this plant is widely used by herbalists. It contains saponins and an astringent substance. Its astringent effect explains why it has been used for ages as a treatment for piles; it makes them contract. The other two herbs principally used by professional herbalists for eczema are yellow dock and burdock. 'Both are what we call "blood cleansers" or alternatives,' Simon Mills explains. 'Admittedly this is a rather vague term, because it is hard to say just what we are supposed to be cleansing from the blood and whether these herbs act on the blood itself at all. It could well be that their main effect is on the digestive tract. But everyday clinical experience shows that they work time and again. In the case of eczema, they usually cause the disease to erupt quite violently for a few days before dying down and clearing up.' The root is the most potent part of both plants and is usually taken internally as a decoction.

Another herb for cuts, bruises, inflammation and piles, which hardly needs any introduction because it is still on the shelves of many a household medical cabinet, is witch hazel, hamamelis. Its leaves and bark are rich in tannins, various bitters and flavonoids, which make it highly astringent and styptic.

For corns and warts the most frequently named remedies are houseleek, dandelion and celandine. The juice from the stalk and/or leaves is applied directly to the affected skin.

Dr Thomson pointed out that almost anything appears to cure warts. Doctors do sometimes cut or burn them off, but they seem to respond equally well to suggestive therapies like hypnosis or bizarre methods like rubbing the wart with bacon fat and then burying the bacon. As the bacon rots, the wart will rot away too – or so the story goes. 'But the remarkable thing is that all the methods have worked,' says Dr Thomson. Both experts agreed that the herbal remedies above would work because these plants have an acid juice which eats the wart or corn away. Dandelion, they suggested, was probably the best.

Wounds

such as deep cuts and bone fractures

More severe wounds call for more vigorous remedies, and in such cases herbalists often turn to comfrey. Such amazing claims have been made for this versatile plant that it is hardly surprising that sceptical outsiders have shown little inclination to take it as seriously as it deserves. The Roman writer Pliny the Elder, for example, describing its wound-healing properties claimed that 'if comfrey root be boiled together with minced meat the meat will at once knit together into a single piece'.

An oil can be extracted from comfrey by macerating the flowering tops of the plant, and this oil is sometimes used to soak the lint under a bandage. Compresses can be made with grated root, or the fresh leaves themselves can be used as a bandage or poultice. Comfrey can also be made into an ointment. Dr Thomson pointed out that any poultice would have a soothing effect on a wound and tend to relieve discomfort.

Simon Mills was more enthusiastic about comfrey. He explained that its wound-healing properties were due to three major constituents of the plant. Firstly it is very rich in tannins which are both astringent and antiseptic. Next, it contains a unique mucilage which forms a putty-like substance when it dries. This protects the wound and draws the edges of a cut together, enabling it to heal more quickly. Thirdly, comfrey contains allantoin, a substance with proven ability to stimulate the growth of connective tissue and bone. Allantoin has the ability to diffuse through the tissues and reach its target quickly.

Though comfrey has been used for centuries, apparently without ill effect, recent research in Australia has revealed that certain varieties of comfrey contain pyrrolizidine alkaloids which can cause liver tumours when fed to animals in large amounts. British herbalists have not been keen to accept that comfrey could be at all dangerous when taken as a medicine, but some scientists believe that it may be undesirable to take it daily as some people do, in the form of a strong infusion.

Comfrey, *Symphytum*

Plants in Pharmacy

Modern medicine sometimes appears to have become so dependent on the synthetic chemicals produced by the pharmaceutical companies that one might be tempted to think that herbal medicines were now just an obsolete relic of the past. This is not true, however, and it may become even less true in the future. There is still certainly a great deal of difference between the technology employed by the research chemists of a major drug company and that of a local herbalist brewing up infusions, decoctions and tinctures. Moreoever there may be disagreements between those who seek to isolate the single most active chemical ingredient of a plant and those who believe (whether for scientific or semi-mystical reasons) that plant medicines should be as close to the natural state of the original plant as possible. Yet despite these differences the pharmaceutical chemists and the herbalists are both drawing on the same source.

This chapter gives a brief profile of some of the principal plants which are used in modern medicine. It is far from being an exhaustive list; others among the dozens which could have been included are aloes, used as purgatives and in lotions for treating burns; cinchona, the source of quinine, used to treat malaria, and quinidine, a heart drug; and ipecacuanha, which is a useful expectorant in small doses and a powerful emetic in larger doses. Medicines from these plants and all the others in this chapter can be found in every doctor's prescribing manuals.

Admittedly some of these medicines are not as popular today as they once were. Colchicine, for instance, is less likely to be prescribed for gout than one of the synthetic anti-inflammatory drugs because of its strong side effects. Rauwolfia and some of the ergot derivatives have fallen out of favour for the same reason, though they are still prescribed. Cocaine is falling behind the newer synthetic local anaesthetics which have less of an effect on the central nervous system, and are not habit forming.

Sometimes, though, the wheel turns full circle. Quinine, for instance, was once the only really potent agent against malaria, but it had been almost completely supplanted by more effective synthetic drugs – until doctors found that certain forms of malaria had become resistant to these new drugs and turned their attention back to quinine which could still help on occasion when the new drugs were of little use. And it will be interesting to see what becomes of cannabis during the next decade or two. A popular medicine in Victorian times, it fell out of medical use around the 1930s when it acquired notoriety as a drug of 'abuse'. Recently, however, it has gained a name as an anti-emetic, very effective at controlling the nausea experienced by patients taking cancer drugs. An American pharmaceutical company has recently managed to create a synthetic drug which has very similar psychic and anti-emetic effects to cannabis: but the experts are now arguing whether they should be using a synthetic drug about which very little is really known, when we have a medicine like cannabis which has been widely used and documented for many years.

Yam
genus *Dioscoreae*

&

Fenugreek
Trigonella foenum-graecum

The tuberous roots of many plants in the 600-strong yam family have been used as food since time immemorial, and are part of the staple diet in Central America and the Caribbean in particular. They are also the greatest source of the hormones used in contraceptive pills, and provide as well raw material for some of the corticosteroids used for relieving pain and inflammation in arthritis, skin conditions and burns.

Yam, genus *Dioscoreae*

A certain amount of the steroids used in the Pill and other sex hormone preparations comes from animal sources or chemical synthesis, but yams still supply the bulk of the pharmaceutical industry's needs. As more than ninety per cent of the hefty yam tubers consists of water, well over 100,000 tonnes of yams have to be harvested every year to provide the 600 or 700 tonnes of the saponin diosgenin used by the drug companies. The yam is a difficult plant to cultivate, and those which are richest in the sought-after steroids take three years to reach maturity. Indeed their cultivation is an art acquired quite recently, and in the early days of production of the Pill most yams were gathered from the wild in Mexico. The Mexican Government, fearful of losing its entire stock of this desirable plant, nationalised the yam industry in 1970. This pushed up prices and made the drug companies look for other sources. India, South Africa and the Far East now supply yams to the industry, though Mexico remains the principal grower.

In China, where Western corticosteroids are regarded as too expensive for widespread medical use, several species of yam are used by the 'barefoot doctors'. Because they are rich in mucilage as well as in anti-inflammatory steroids, decoctions of root and powdered root are used for gastro-intestinal inflammation and for treating rheumatoid arthritis.

Although the yam supply is not in any immediate danger of disappearing, the high cost of yams has encouraged researchers to seek other sources of diosgenin, and one of the most interesting of these is fenugreek, *Trigonella foenum-graecum*. *Foenum-graecum* is Latin for Greek hay, another of the plant's names and one which reminds us of its history as a culinary and medicinal herb in the Mediterranean. Though the Greeks knew nothing about sex hormones they seem to have been the first to exploit fenugreek's hormonal richness. Dr W.A.R. Thomson reports that it used to be used to improve the roundness of women's breasts and to stimulate the flow of breast milk, though this may have been due more to its high protein content.

The Agricultural Research Council has been funding the research of a Bath University pharmacist, Dr Roland Hardman, who has spent more than ten years developing species of fenugreek which will yield large amounts of diosgenin. Fenugreek may well become a popular crop with European farmers, because as well as providing diosgenin from its seeds, the rest of the plant provides animal fodder and the seed oil can also be used for flavouring foods. Fenugreek also restores nitrogen to the soil, making it a useful rotation crop.

Madagascan periwinkle
Vinca rosea

Vinca rosea and its botanical cousin, *Vinca major*, had an old reputation as a cure for diabetes. Research pharmacists interested in seeing whether the periwinkle might provide an alternative to insulin tested various preparations and extracts of the plants but failed to substantiate the old herbalists' claims. However, in their research they did discover something just as remarkable, that the Madagascan periwinkle had potent anti-cancer properties. An American drug company isolated two alkaloids from the plant, vincristine and vinblastine, which are now an important part of standard therapy for Hodgkin's disease, childhood leukaemia and other forms of cancer. These diseases were once almost certain killers and still are responsible for many young deaths, though many lives have been saved with the help of these herbal alkaloids.

However the alkaloids are extracted at great cost; up to fifteen tons of periwinkle leaves are needed to produce a single ounce. The isolated chemical is extremely potent; only a few milligrammes are administered at a time.

Mayapple
Podophyllum peltatum
&
Mistletoe
Viscum album

In recent years the National Cancer Institute in the United States has been testing thousands of plants annually for potential anti-tumour properties. Though the results have numerically been rather disappointing – out of about 100,000 extracts from about 30,000 plants, about 3,000 have revealed some kind of anti-tumour activity but only fifteen have got as far as tentative clinical trials – a few plants examined by the National Cancer Institute do look promising.

Madagascan periwinkle, *Vinca rosea*

They found that the roots of the mayapple, *Podophyllum peltatum*, used by North American Indians as a purgative, contain a toxin which prevents leukaemic and certain other cancer cells from replicating.

Mistletoe, *Viscum album*, a holy plant for the Druids and ascribed all kinds of magical and medicinal properties throughout the ages, also contains several proteins with anti-tumour activity, though the results of early clinical trials were not enough to convince the medical profession and drug industry that it was worth developing mistletoe further as a cancer drug. Nevertheless, homoeopathic doctors regard mistletoe as a potent anti-cancer plant and use it in minute doses in a remedy called iscador.

Foxglove
Digitalis purpurea

The foxglove has an interesting and well-documented history as a medicinal plant. In 1775 a Birmingham physician, William Withering, was told by one of his patients of a medicine she had been given by a Shropshire 'wise woman' for treating her dropsy. It was a strange brew containing bits and bobs from various plants. Dr Withering, impressed by the fact that his patient had actually got better and lost much of her oedema (retained water) after taking the wise woman's medicine, investigated the remedy for himself and identified the most important herbal ingredient as foxglove root. Subsequent tests on his patients revealed that the leaves, gathered when the plant was in full bloom, were by far the most potent part of the plant for curing dropsy. Dr Withering's book *An Account of the Foxglove*, which he published in 1785 reported how he had tested his foxglove preparations on scores of patients, and as well as becoming a classic medical text, the book set the standard of medicinal research for years to come. Dr Withering did not discover what we know now, that the active principles of digitalis are certain glycosides which act on the heart muscle. Dropsy is often the result of defective heart-muscle action; the blood is not flushed vigorously enough through the system to carry away the fluid which accumulates in the tissues. By strengthening and regularising the pumping heart, the excess fluids are swept out through the kidneys.

Foxglove, *Digitalis purpurea*

Digitalis was prescribed by doctors in tincture or powder form, sometimes as raw leaf, to be chewed, for congestive heart failure. By the 1930s it had attracted the attention of drug companies who were keen to isolate its active principles to make it into a patentable medicine which could be given in standardised doses and by intravenous injection.

The glycosides digoxin and digitoxin were identified, but although these isolated principles had a quicker action than the old digitalis preparations and could be given in injections in emergencies, it was only after their introduction that digitalis poisoning became a regular side effect of medical treatment. Doctors found that although they were prescribing purer substances, individual requirements differed greatly from patient to patient and the drug also tended to accumulate in the body, so it was all too easy, sometimes fatally so, to give an overdose. Digitalis derivatives are, of course, still widely prescribed today, though accumulation and side effects are still a major hazard.

Dr W.A.R. Thomson is a physican who believes that his colleagues should be returning their attention to herbal medicines, and cites digoxin as an example of how the drug companies have, in his opinion, been rash to assume that an isolated chemical is a better medicine than the whole herb.

> *'In nine cases out of ten the patient did not need the kind of rapid action you get from digoxin, and although you could overdose from taking digitalis leaf this did not happen with anything like the regularity we experienced with the isolated glycosides. The drug companies found a market largely because digitalis preparations, especially the tinctures, had got a name for unreliability. This was simply due to the fact that the chemists tended to keep them on their shelves too long until they had lost much of their power. But this could have been avoided by using the powdered form of digitalis prepared to the British Pharmacopoeia standards.'*

Thus he believes a good herbal medicine was largely lost. Herbalists are no longer allowed to prescribe digitalis unless they are qualified doctors or pharmacists.

Indian snakeroot
Rauwolfia serpentina

Rauwolfia, like Digitalis, is another medicinal herb which herbalists are no longer allowed to prescribe because as well as being a medicine it can have dangerous toxic effects in overdosage. Used for centuries in India for sedating excited maniacs, snakeroot alkaloids gained attention for their ability to lower blood pressure in the 1940s. Indian chemists and doctors were the first to examine snakeroot for its active principles and their clinical effect, but once reports of its effectiveness against high blood pressure were published in the *British Heart Journal* and other publications in 1949, the European drug companies became very interested in the plant – so much so that the Indian government had to ban all export of snakeroot because all the natural supplies were being bought up. As well as reducing blood pressure it has a tranquillising effect, which made the drug companies even more interested in it.

The main active principle isolated from the root is the alkaloid reserpine. Reserpine has fallen from popularity with doctors during the last decade because of its side effects, which at low doses include drowsiness and vertigo and at high doses slowing of the heartbeat and depression. Herbalists argue that it was a mistake for chemists to isolate reserpine from the snakeroot and that they should have stuck with the whole plant which was not known to cause severe side effects when taken in infusions. (Gandhi used to take snakeroot tea as a nightcap.) In many ways its history as a medicinal plant resembles that of Digitalis.

Ergot
Claviceps purpurea

Ergot is really a fungus which grows on rye. Though it contains various substances which are useful to the medical prescriber, in the Middle Ages it was the cause of an appalling plague known as St Anthony's Fire. Anyone who consumed rye which had been con-

Indian snakeroot, *Rauwolfia serpentina*

taminated with the ergot fungus was liable to suffer from the disease, and it was not uncommon for whole towns or villages to fall victim. The symptoms of St Anthony's Fire were convulsions and hallucinations along with burning pains in the hands and feet, and subsequent gangrene.

Ergot contains more than a dozen potent alkaloids which between them have an enormous range of action. The most famous, indeed notorious, of these is lysergic acid, the base for lysergic acid diethylamide 25, better known as LSD. The hallucinogenic properties of LSD were first experienced by a Swiss pharmacologist, Dr Albert Hofmann, who had been isolating the active principles of ergot and testing their effect for a Swiss drug company. During his early laboratory experiments with LSD he found himself transported into a strange, disassociated dream-like state, and wondered whether this had anything to do with the new substance in his test tubes. To find out, he took what he thought would be the minimum dose necessary to achieve an effect, a quarter of a milligramme. He was soon to discover that this dose was ten times as much as anyone needed to experience all the full-blown, florid visions of heaven and hell, transcendent beauty and terrors which have been described by many authors, such as Aldous Huxley's account in *The Doors of Perception*. Poor Dr Hofmann saw the world crumble around him, he felt as though his soul had left his body, at one stage of his trip he looked down from the ceiling to see his corpse lying on the sofa.

The amazing properties of this ergot derivative attracted psychiatrists, who wondered whether it would get their patients to travel back into the obscure reaches of their 'subconscious', and it is even said that officers of the Central Intelligence Agency thought it might be a 'truth drug', which they could administer to taciturn captives. It proved pretty useless in this latter capacity but doctors still use it with discrimination on carefully selected patients and for experimental purposes. It is also largely used by non-law-abiding seekers of instant visions.

More significant medically are the ergot derivatives ergometrine and ergotamine. The former exerts a powerful effect on the muscle of the womb, making its contractions strong, and is therefore used to assist women in childbirth and to check postpartum haemorrhage, the bleeding which sometimes follows delivery. Ergotamine also acts on the womb, but its main application is in the treatment of migraine. By interfering with the endings of sympathetic nerves it causes blood vessels to constrict, thus checking the excessive flow of

Ergot, *Claviceps purpurea*, growing on rye

Two varieties of the opium poppy, *Papaver somniferum*

blood to the brain which is often the cause of migraine headaches.

Another drug derived from ergot, bromocriptine, is used to treat Parkinson's disease, because it stimulates nerve endings in the brain known as dopamine receptors. It also acts on the pituitary gland, discouraging it from releasing prolactin and growth hormone. This hormonal action has made the drug useful in the treatment of prostate problems in men, excessive lactation in women, and in acromegaly, a disorder in which hands, head and feet grow too large.

Opium poppy
Papaver somniferum

Opium is perhaps the most famous and notorious herbal medicine of all, and the source of pain-killing drugs which have not been superseded by any synthetic. The black, sticky opium paste with its strange smell, both acrid and sweet, is still used as a medicine in parts of Turkey and Iran where it grows.

It is of course narcotic, but very good at controlling gut spasms and diarrhoea. Laudanum, the tincture which used to be sold over the counter by pharmacists well into the last century, was the only really effective pain-killer available to surgeons and those who cared for the dying. A purified opium extract, papaveretum, is still used as a pain-killer, and contains a mixture of the many alkaloids which come from the seed pods of the plant. Though many people probably do not realise it, codeine is an opium alkaloid with similar effects to morphine, though much milder. As well as relieving pain through its direct action on the central nervous system, morphine and the related opium alkaloids reduce the cough reflex and act on the muscles of the gut. These two actions can be useful if the patient happens to be suffering from a cough or diarrhoea, but they are just as often an unwanted side effect. Constipation can become a problem for patients taking even small doses of these drugs, and morphine's tendency to depress the part of the brain which keeps us breathing can present real hazards if the patient is weak and semi- or unconscious. Diamorphine, better known as heroin, is quicker and shorter acting than morphine, but the risks of addiction are greater.

In the United States, where the fear of drug addiction has

produced an overreaction by politicians against heroin, this drug is not even available to doctors, though a public campaign is now being waged to have it made available to doctors who look after patients with chronic cancer pain. Though doctors in this country have been taught to fear addiction and tolerance (the need for ever-increasing doses to achieve the same effect), those who specialise in the care of cancer patients and others with chronic painful disease have found that if dosage is kept at the optimum level in each individual – just enough to relieve pain, but not enough to cause drowsiness or confusion – and given at regular intervals before the underlying pain makes itself felt again, then tolerance and addiction are a minor problem when set against the pain relief obtained by the patient.

Two other opium alkaloids are used in modern medicine: papaverine, which relaxes smooth (that is, internal) muscles and is therefore used to relieve colic and bronchial asthma, and noscapine, an effective cough suppressant which does not relieve pain and has little if any effect on mood.

Ma-huang
Ephedra vulgaris

A shrub which grows in northern China, ephedra has been part of Chinese medicine for centuries. The knobbly stems and branches were used in infusions to relieve chest complaints and as a tonic. Its effectiveness as a medicine attracted the interest of chemists almost a hundred years ago, and in 1885 a Japanese scientist isolated its main active principle, ephedrine. Ephedrine acts in very much the same way as adrenaline; it stimulates the sympathetic nervous system, increasing blood pressure and opening the airways round the lung. It was not until about fifty years ago that ephedrine gained the attention of the European medical profession, but since then it has proved to be a valuable treatment for asthma. The great advantage of ephedrine over adrenaline is that it can be taken by mouth, whereas adrenaline has to be injected.

Herbalists argue that this is another example of a plant which has more desirable therapeutic effects in its natural state than when its active principle has been extracted and used by itself. One of the drawbacks of ephedrine is the fact that it raises blood pressure. Herbalists point out that there is no record of infusions of the whole plant causing high blood pressure even though it has all the beneficial effects of ephedrine alone. They suggest that plant infusions may be safer because they contain a number of other alkaloids and substances, like pseudo ephedrine, which 'buffer' the effects of the main active principle. No one appears to have done clinical trials to compare the effects of ephedra infusions and ephedrine directly, however, so it is a moot point whether one is more beneficial or has fewer side effects than the other. Ephedra roots can be bought in some Chinese shops in Britain; they are also imported by some medical herbalists.

Coca
Erythroxylum coca

Though cocaine is now a proscribed drug, hedged around with as many legal penalties as heroin and LSD (which have arguably contributed to its popularity rather than put pleasure seekers off it), it was once freely available as a medicine and an ingredient of numerous pep-up tonics which were sold over the counter in pharmacies and grocery stores. In the British Library there are thirteen volumes of testimonials devoted to one of the most commercially successful of these tonics, known as Mariani's Coca Wine. A highly aromatic blend of coca leaf extracts and wine, this invigorating brew was supped by, among others, Thomas Edison, H. G. Wells, Jules Verne, Emile Zola, the American President McKinley and Louis Blériot, who took a flask of it with him when he flew the English Channel in 1909. Pope Leo XIII awarded its inventor, Angelo Mariani, a gold medal for his tonic which, according to Mariani's biographer, His Holiness took daily to keep him going through the autumn of his life. Less than a hundred years ago Dr Sigmund Freud was using cocaine himself, and recommending it to patients and colleagues alike. He found that it calmed his jittery stomach as well as stimulating thought. It also seems to have been a powerful aphrodisiac, for in 1884 he wrote to his fiancée:

Coca, *Erythroxylum coca*

> *'Woe to you, my Princess, when I come. I will kiss you quite red and feed you until you are plump. And if you willfully resist, you shall see who is the stronger, a gentle little girl who doesn't eat enough or a big wild man with cocaine in his body.'*

Once reserved for the privileged members of Inca society, coca leaves are now chewed by the poorest South American Indians of Bolivia and Peru to keep them buoyant in their drudgery. Cocaine is only one of the many alkaloids and bitter and aromatic principles to be found in coca leaf, several of which have stimulant and/or anaesthetic properties.

Cocaine, which was first isolated in 1860, was an enormous breakthrough in anaesthetics and undoubtedly relieved a vast amount of suffering through its potent local anaesthetic properties. It has been largely superseded as a local anaesthetic by synthetic compounds, like lignocaine, which can be given by injection. Cocaine is not injected for medical purposes because it causes such violent stimulation of the central nervous system. Cocaine eye drops are still used by opthalmologists, and cocaine powder is used by some cosmetic surgeons: before performing operations on the nose, for instance, they pack it with cocaine, then break the bone with a silver hammer. Cocaine also used to be an ingredient of the so-called Brompton Cocktail, a mixture of heroin or morphine with a sedative and/or alcohol, given to patients suffering from painful terminal illness. Cocaine was put into these 'cocktails' both as a pain-killer and as a stimulant to overcome the depressive effects of the other ingredients of the mixture, but now that specialists in terminal care are more expert in prescribing pain-killers like morphine without making the patient too drowsy, cocaine has been dropped from the recipe in most hospitals.

Deadly nightshade, *Atropa belladonna*

Deadly Nightshade
Atropa belladonna

Henbane
Hyoscyamus niger
&
Thorn-apple
Datura stramonium

These three plants contain alkaloids which are chemically related –
atropine, hyoscine and hyoscyamine – which have a potent effect on
the nervous system. Belladonna, 'the beautiful lady', is so called
because it used to be dropped into the eyes of courtly ladies (and is
still used by rather less courtly ladies in the Mediterranean) to make
their pupils dilate in a decadent, enticing fashion. It is in fact rather
dangerous to use atropine in this way, because doing it too often can
cause glaucoma. It is also allergenic; some people can get skin rashes
or conjunctivitis (pink eye) from it. In smaller doses atropine is a
stimulant, causing excitement and restlessness, and in large doses it
can provoke hallucinations and delirium, which explains why it was
popular with witches and others who sought visionary experiences
through drugs. Like hyoscine and hyoscyamine, it 'switches off' the
parasympathetic nervous system, which is the division of the nervous system that, among other things, slows the heart beat, increases
gut movement and stimulates activity in the secretory organs which
produce tears, saliva and sweat. Atropine is therefore used mechani-
cally to dry up these secretions before an operation so that the
anaesthetised patient does not drown in his or her own mucus.
Because of its effect on the parasympathetic nervous system it is also
useful for controlling spasms in the gastro-intestinal tract and is an
aid in the treatment of peptic ulcers. It can also reduce the muscular
rigidity and excessive salivation suffered by people with Parkinson's
disease. Atropine and related drugs are also used in medicines for
relieving air, car and sea sickness.

Thorn-apple, *Datura stramonium*

Growing Useful Plants

It might have been all very well for witches to creep out to the crossroads at midnight to collect their herbs, but this is not a practical proposition today. Unless you are lucky enough to live in a rural area where the farmers don't use insecticides or weed-killers and where the passing motorists do not sully the banks and hedgerows with lead and other pollutants in their exhaust fumes, collecting herbs from the side of the road is downright dangerous.

Herbs which are going to be eaten, applied to your skin or taken as a medicine should obviously not be contaminated with toxic chemicals. So we have to resort to specialist herb farmers or grow the stuff ourselves. Large and learned books are available which give detailed advice about cultivating herbs and they cannot be rivalled by a little book like this. But at least I can outline some basic principles and pass on, in brief, a few tips from the experts I consulted during the series.

Many popular herbs are not indigenous to Britain and may be more trouble than native species. Basil, for instance, is a Mediterranean herb which needs plenty of sun. Some herbs need hardly any looking-after at all; yarrow, mint and borage are self-propagating and can rapidly become a weed. Some, like thyme, prefer a well-drained, light soil, whereas others, like dandelion, will thrive on heavy clay. It's also worth bearing in mind how tall your herbs are going to grow; obviously you should not plant short herbs like thyme or parsley behind some tall angelica or next to some rambling, space-hungry nasturtium.

Generally speaking, aromatic herbs do not suffer from the depredations of insects as much as other plants. Indeed, infusions of certain herbs make a good repellent spray. Garlic is one of the best in this respect; in fact, if garlic is planted near other species it will often protect them from insects. A maceration of stinging nettles in rain water will also get rid of many insects, and it is very nutritious for plants too.

Aromatic herbs like the sun, so reserve a bright spot for thyme, sage, rosemary and lavender. Herbs which can thrive in more shady places include angelica, chervil, celery, lady's mantle, lungwort, marsh-mallow, parsley and hypericum, St John's wort, which produces bright yellow flowers with little exposure to direct sunlight.

Two herbs whose popularity is only equalled by the difficulty they present to the grower are parsley and basil. Growers have come up with an intriguing variety of excuses for their failure with parsley. According to various superstitions it will not grow if the husband is not master of his house, if the grower is not a honest man, or if it was not planted on Good Friday. The seeds are said to have to go to the Devil and back nine times before they germinate. One way of softening up parsley seeds to accelerate germination is to pour boiling water over them. Germinate the seeds in a greenhouse and take care when planting out the seedlings, as they are quite delicate. They are best planted out in a semi-shaded place. Basil calls for a delicate balance of warmth and moisture. The seeds will not germinate till the earth is getting warm, usually around May, and when the seedlings do pop up they will probably be eaten by slugs before you set eyes on them. Perhaps the simplest course of action is to buy small established plants from a professional grower. Once planted out they need sun and plenty of moisture; but don't leave them too wet or they will develop fungus at the base of their stem. Basil has an Italian temperament: a single leaf will perfume a salad like no native British herb. A note of warning though – basil will be wiped out by the first touch of frost.

I asked Heinz Zeylstra, principal of the National Institute of Medical Herbalists' college and an experienced herb grower, to name the six herbs he would cultivate if he were not allowed to grow more than six, and which he thought would be the most useful. He named yarrow, dandelion, peppermint, valerian, chamomile and hops, and offered some advice about how to grow them:

Yarrow, *Achillea millefolium* (which is a febrifuge, purgative and astringent on the skin) presents no problems. It is a roadside and pasture weed and will grow in virtually any soil. The leaves and flowers are most potent when the plant has been in bloom for a week.

Dandelion, *Taraxacum officinale* (a diuretic and rich in potassium), is of course also very hardy. But if you have only seen dandelions growing in a lawn, you would be amazed by the eighteen-inch-tall and two-foot wide specimens which can be cultivated if the plant is given space and kept free of weeds. Heinz Zeylstra has collected a pound of leaves from a single plant. The leaves can be picked for salads all the year round; the medicinal value of the root is at its highest in early spring or late autumn.

Peppermint, *Mentha piperita*, whose volatile oils are antiseptic and help relax spasm in the airways, is another Mediterranean species which needs the sun if it is to produce its sweet-smelling principles. Mints grow naturally in damp places, so in a garden they need to be kept well watered, and grown in a soil which does not drain too quickly. It propagates itself by sending out creepers just under the ground. Like the garden mint used for flavouring lamb it will live for years, but it tends to get patchy and is best replaced every two or three years. The leaves are richest in oil just before the plant comes into full flower.

Valerian, *Valeriana officinalis*, which used to be a standard prescription for 'nerves', contains its active principles largely in its roots. Its roots are bushy and fine so it needs to be cultivated in a lightish soil so that the roots can be easily extracted from the earth. Its natural environment is damp, boggy places, and the plant needs plenty of water and shade. It is best to leave the plant in the same place for two or three years to let the root system develop fully. It should be harvested in the autumn when the upper parts of the plant have started to die away.

Chamomile, *Matricaria chamomilla*, has a wide range of medicinal uses which include the relief of flatulence or dyspepsia, childhood asthma and inflammation. It is a vigorous wild flower which appears in banks and on rubbish tips and is widely cultivated in Europe. Chamomile tea, made from an infusion of the flowers, is a very popular national drink in Germany and Italy. Seeds can be bought from most herb dealers and are best germinated in a seed tray before being planted out in rich, dryish soil which is not too heavy. The active principles are at their strongest in the flowers about a week after they have bloomed. Removing the flowers encourages more to grow in their place: so with chamomile you can have your herb and drink it.

Hops, *Humulus lupulus*, whose flowers have a reputation for being an aphrodisiac for women but sexually quietening for men, is more generally used as an aid against insomnia (in hop pillows) and as a stomach relaxant. The traditional area for hop growing in England is Kent, where most brewers get their supplies. It is a climbing plant which will grow up to six metres on a framework of poles. It will grow in most soils, but a rich one is best. It is also a plant with two forms: male and female; it is the cone-shaped flowers of the female which contain the active principles. They are harvested in late August or early September.

Cooking and Drying

In the old royal courts of India the physician was more than a dispenser of drugs and medical advice; he was also in charge of the kitchens, supervising his master's menu and deciding what diets should be followed at particular times of the year. One practical reason for having the physician in the kitchen was to ensure that the king was not poisoned, but it was thought just as important that he should advise the cooks how to keep the royal humours in balance. In the summer, for instance, he would recommend 'cooling' foods and beverages to counteract the prevailing heat. In the rainy season, when 'wind' was the prevailing element, he would recommend sweet, acid and salty-tasting foods which, according to the traditional theory, counteracted the influence of wind.

Some advice offered by those Indian physicians might not go down too well in Western medical circles today. Pregnancy, for example, was regarded as a 'hot' condition and mothers-to-be were discouraged from eating meat, eggs and other protein-rich foods which were also 'hot'.

In European cuisine, herbs are used more for their flavours and colours than for health reasons, but it is worth remembering that they can be a valuable source of vitamins and trace elements, especially if they are eaten fresh and raw. Watercress and parsley contain trace amounts of manganese, iodine and iron; nettles are particularly rich in iron too, and herbs are a source of vitamin C.

Alfalfa, which has been used for centuries as cattle fodder, is now enjoying increasing popularity as a kitchen herb and vegetable, is rich in many vitamins which can seldom be found together in the same food: they include vitamins A, B12, E, K and niacin. Cooking, particularly the English habit of boiling vegetables to a near pulp, is one of the best ways of destroying vitamins; so it would be no exaggeration to say that the sprig of fresh herb, which so many people seem to think is just a garnish to be left on the side of the plate, often contains as much vitamin as the cooked meal.

For advice on the best ways in which to use herbs in the kitchen I consulted a variety of experts including Anton Mossiman, *maître chef des cuisines* at the Dorchester Hotel in London; Gail Duff, cookery writer and student of country lore; Tom Vernon, broadcaster and bon viveur; and Ruth Thompson, a herb grower. All agreed that fresh herbs collected from the garden really could never be equalled by the dried herbs you might buy in a shop. When herbs are dried they inevitably lose much of the volatile oils which give them their scent and flavour, and the longer they are stored the more flavour they will lose. If you are obliged to resort to dried herbs from a shop you will find that you need two or three times as much dried herb as you would fresh herb to achieve a similar effect on the palate. In the case of basil, which Mossiman and Vernon independently declared to be the very finest of the *fines herbes*, there is just no comparison between the fresh and dried versions; the subtler fragrances just evaporate altogether when basil is dried.

So what is the poor cook to do in winter time when the garden is barren and bare? Well, some herbs do survive the British winter quite well if they are not too exposed. Sage, rosemary and thyme may not be throwing out fresh leaves in midwinter, but they do keep going. If they have been allowed to grow big enough in the warm months, they should be able to put up with a bit of cropping in the winter. With rosemary, care should be taken not to break off the stems of the plant, otherwise frost will penetrate into it. Winter savory, as its name implies, is very hardy too, though rather woodier than the summer savory.

'Cooking is a seasonal activity, and these herbs which survive in the cold months go very well with the casseroles, stews and hot meats we eat in winter,' Gail Duff pointed out.

Anton Mossiman suggested that most kitchen herbs had a much better flavour before they had come into full bloom. And he recommended that anyone who might not be able to get hold of fresh herbs at certain times of the year should collect them at their prime and freeze them immediately, either in foil, a plastic bag or in a little yoghourt carton. 'Freezing is far better than drying.'

If you don't have a freezer, drying your herbs may be the only option. The experts described their own drying methods, which differ slightly in detail. Tom Vernon dries his herbs on a mesh or sieve in the sun and open air. In a hot summer rosemary and thyme will dry themselves out on the stalk and can be bottled straight way, though this form of natural drying may be more reliable in Mediterranean climates than in most parts of Britain. Gail Duff ties her herbs into small bunches and hangs them up in the airing cupboard for a week. Ruth Thompson agreed that herbs were best dried in a dark place so that they did not lose their colour, but she thought the airing cupboard would not be warm enough; she opts for a rack above a boiler or range, out of the direct sunlight and with plenty of circulating air.

Drying herbs in the oven is a risky business because the water and oils in the herb can evaporate too fast. The general consensus was that if the oven had to be used, then it should be set at the lowest possible setting, perhaps even with the oven door open (if your oven can be operated safely this way), and the herbs should not be left in for more than a couple of hours at the most.

Another alternative is to put your herbs into vinegar. This is one way of preserving basil, so that even if you cannot have a fresh basil leaf in winter you can at least enjoy its delicate flavours. You make it before the September frosts, simply by poking sprigs of the herb into a bottle of white wine vinegar and leaving it to macerate for two or three weeks on a sunny windowsill.

As the English language is so bereft of words to describe scents and flavours, books and radio programmes are not much use for conveying the individual virtues of the different culinary herbs. You can compare some herbs to one another: the aniseed taste of fennel, for instance, or fresh borage which tastes rather like a cucumber with bristles. However, the only practical advice one can offer about choosing herbs to suit your palate is: try them for yourself.

One of the most important things to decide is whether you want the flavour of the herbs to dominate a dish or to make a more gentle contribution. For mushrooms, which have a very delicate flavour, Tom Vernon recommended 'the tiniest sprig of rosemary'. Marjoram will give a very distinctive taste to a salad – delicious if you have not tried it before but perhaps not the kind of thing you would want every day of the week. Anton Mossiman agreed that herbs should not be overdone and that a leg of lamb would only need to be flavoured with a single herb, rosemary, and that a sauce for white fish need only contain basil or chervil. Stronger meats call out for stronger flavours, however, and in his book *Cuisine à la Carte*

Mossiman gives a list of twenty-two herbs and spices which he mixes together to add to *foie gras*. They are nutmeg, cloves, bay leaves, white pepper, black pepper, cinnamon, ginger, cardamon, marjoram, coriander, basil, mace, thyme, juniper berries, curry powder, tarragon, chervil, rosemary, pepper leaves, cayenne, dill and ground fennel! And for a rich fish like monkfish, he recommends marinating the fish for eight to ten hours in olive oil with a mixture of fresh basil, chervil, chives, parsley, thyme and rosemary.

Unlike some cooks who like to chop their herbs up so fine that you could not tell from looking that they were there at all, Mossiman prefers to leave them as whole as possible 'so that you can see what you are eating'.

Herbs need not be confined to vegetables and meat dishes. Elderflowers, sweet cicely and angelica take some of the tartness from apple and other fruit dishes and add something of their own. Leaves from scented geraniums aromatise milk dishes; and Ruth Thompson suggested putting one or two leaves on the bottom of a Victoria sandwich cake tin before you pour the mixture in, as it adds an interesting and unusual flavour. Candied angelica, of course, can be used for cakes too; Ruth Thompson advises that if you want to preserve your own angelica you should take the young stems of the plant as they come up in the spring, dunk them in boiling syrup, let them dry on greaseproof paper, then repeat this once a day for another day or two until they are thick and stiff. Tom Vernon spoke of a traditional savoury custard from Worcestershire made with marigold petals and thyme which was served up with apple tart and roast pork. And Anton Mossiman described how he had been asked to think up a sorbet which would not be too sweet and could be eaten between courses. He made the sorbet from tomatoes, but found at the last minute that it still had a rather strong and acid taste. This was perfectly remedied by adding fresh basil leaves.

You can also experiment with different species of the same herb. Tom Vernon and Ruth Thompson both preferred the flat-leaved continental parsley to the curly-leaved variety which is more often seen in Britain, both for its flavour and because it was easier to grow. There are many species of mint too. Ruth Thompson recommended peppermint for teas, eau-de-Cologne mint for potpourri and summer drinks, curled mint for lamb and apple mint for new potatoes. But of course there are no rules to this game; it's all a matter of taste.

Herbal Cosmetics

Herbal cosmetics, skin cleansers and other 'beauty products' lie thick on the shelves of shops today. Many 'herbal' shampoos and creams contain only a tiny amount of herbal material to give them colour or perfume. And some products which one might rashly assume to contain herbs contain no plant material at all. The word 'lemon' in a brand name does not have to mean that the product has any lemon in it, the lemon-like smell could come from some purely synthetic additive.

During my research for the radio series I asked the public analyst of a large county authority how we might set about analysing a sample of herbal cosmetics to find out what they really did contain. He replied that his department did not have the means to buy the gas chromatographer and mass spectrometer equipment necessary for performing such an analysis. So even if the laws about manufacturing and labelling herbal cosmetics were tightened up, few local authorities would be able to enforce them. 'It would seem that the manufacturers of these herbal products have a "potential licence for abuse" as the sometimes extravagant claims cannot be checked.'

A good reason for trying herbal cosmetics rather than the more conventional ones might be that you suffer from allergies. Cosmetics and perfumes are a major cause of dermatitis on the face, and some people are highly sensitive to certain chemicals. A herbal alternative could offer a solution, but you can only find out by trying it, for allergy to plants is probably just as common as chemical allergy. Among the plants which are known to have caused allergies at some time or other are: cinnamon, vanilla, cassia, peppermint, caraway, nettles, and henna. All these herbs are used in various beauty products, plus lanolin, which is a particularly common allergen.

However, only about one person in ten is allergy-prone, so this warning should not be taken to mean that these substances are to be avoided by everyone.

Gail Duff, actress Suzy Kendall and model Pat Wellington gave me a number of simple beauty treatments which are genuinely herbal, can be made at home and have been tried by them personally. Unlike most commercial products these treatments prepared in your home will not of course contain preservatives (another common source of allergies), but by the same token they should be kept only for a short time even in a refrigerator, because they are organic and offer an attractive environment for bacteria.

Bath oils

You can scent your bathwater with a homemade bath oil which smells as good as the most expensive brands but costs a tenth of the price by adding a few drops of essential oil to a pint of baby oil. Make up your own recipes by mixing different essential oils: some of the best for this purpose are jasmine, bergamot, tobacco, lavender and rose (Musk too, though it is not a herb.) You will need to rinse the oil from the bath afterwards, but it is very good for your skin. You only need about a tablespoonful per bath.

Face packs

Simmer 454gm (1lb) of fresh nettles in 1cm ($\frac{1}{2}$in) of water for about quarter of an hour. The cooking destroys the stinging formic acid, so have no fear of placing the resulting green mush on a piece of muslin and applying the pack to your face for 15 minutes. Wash the nettles off with water and lemon juice (GD).

Pulped apples or crushed strawberries also make a delicately pleasant-smelling mask. Wash them off with an elderflower infusion or cleanser (see above).

Skin cleanser

Simmer six teaspoonfuls of elderflower blossoms in 275ml ($\frac{1}{2}$ pint) of milk for half an hour. Take it off the heat, cover it, and leave it to cool for three hours before straining it and putting the liquid in the fridge (SK, PW).

Spots and blackheads

These may be improved by putting your head under a towel and holding your face about a foot above a strong hot infusion of sage or thyme, which contain antiseptic volatile oils. Don't hold your face too close to boiling water, though, because you might burst some of the fine blood vessels in your face.

Hair

Hair seems to respond well to a number of herbs, notably nettles and rosemary. A herbal oil made by steeping rosemary in olive oil for a few weeks can be rubbed into the scalp, then rinsed out. Alternatively, make a decoction of nettles and comb a handful of the liquid into your hair. Both these recipes are widely acclaimed to clear up dandruff. Rinses of infusions of chamomile, marigold or sage are also good for keeping the scalp clean and healthy; all these herbs are used in various skin preparations made by herbalists.

Finally, if you want an original and entirely herbal cosmetic which will make you stand out from the crowd, how about woad? A tall plant (it grows about three feet high) and not difficult to grow in your garden, it has pretty yellow flowers and is the source of the blue dye which ancient Britons used to put on their faces and dye their scanty clothes with. The leaves are astringent and styptic, so the Briton only had to dab a little more on if he was wounded – and no one would notice the difference. The perfect war paint for all social occasions – and a direct link with our herbal past.

Glossary

Plants contain an enormous array of substances, proteins, enzymes, phenols, vitamins, salts, cellulose, glycosides, chlorophyll and trace elements being some of the major ones. When a pharmaceutical chemist investigates a plant, he usually tries to identify the substance or substances having the most marked effect on living organisms, and most of the plant-based medicines produced by the drug companies consist of these *active principles* rather than the whole herb. Herbalists often argue that this approach is wrong, and that plants contain so many substances which act together that it is not possible to get as good a medicine from isolated active principles as you can get from the whole plant. This is arguable, but it certainly is true that few plants have been examined in such detail that scientists have been able to identify all their chemical ingredients.

A brief explanation is given overleaf of some of the types of chemical compound often found in herbs and of some other terms which appear in the text.

Abortifacient induces abortion

Alkaloid organic compounds from plants which contain at least one nitrogen atom in the molecule

Analgesic reduces pain

Astringent closes the pores and checks discharge of fluid from tissues

Bitters bitter-tasting substances extracted from herbs, usually by soaking the herb in alcohol. Simple bitters stimulate the palate as well as the production of digestive acids in the stomach. Aromatic bitters also have a strong aroma

Carminative relieves colicky or griping pains and expels wind (gas) from the stomach and gut

Flavonoids plant proteins, usually aromatic and yellow coloured

Diuretic increases the flow of urine

Emetic makes you vomit

Emmenagogue encourages menstruation. Often used as euphemism for 'abortifacient'

Expectorant expels mucus from the airways

Glycoside organic substance consisting of a sugar combined with another molecule

Laxative relieves constipation

Mucilage gelatinous material which absorbs water

Narcotic induces sleep or stupor. Sometimes 'narcotic' is inaccurately used to describe any intoxicating drug, whether stimulant (like cocaine) or soporific (like morphine)

Purgative clears out the gut

Saponin substance which acts like a soap or detergent

Styptic checks bleeding

Tannin Complex natural compounds which contain acids, phenols, glycosides. Tannins have an astringent effect

Useful Books and Addresses

I have found these books useful:

A Modern Herbal, by Mrs M. Grieve, PENGUIN

Healing Plants: a Modern Herbal, edited by W.A.R. Thomson, MACMILLAN

The Barefoot Doctor's Manual, prepared by the Revolutionary Health Committee of Hunan Province, ROUTLEDGE AND KEGAN PAUL

The Herb and Spice Book by Sarah Garland, FRANCES LINCOLN-WEIDENFELD AND NICOLSON

Books by contributors mentioned in the text:

Herbs That Heal, by W.A.R. Thomson, A & C BLACK

Country Wisdom, by Gail Duff, PAN

Cuisine à la Carte, by Anton Mossiman, NORTHWOOD BOOKS

Natural Appeal, by Suzy Kendall and Pat Wellington, DENT

Useful addresses:

The Herb Society
34 Boscobel Place, London SW1W 9PE
Telephone 01–235 1530

Formerly called *The Society of Herbalists*, this is now a society for professionals and amateurs with an interest in useful plants. It publishes *The Herbal Review*, which includes articles by acknowledged experts on growing, cooking, herbal medicines and herbal history as well as names and addresses of many herb farms and suppliers of herbs.

National Institute of Medical Herbalists
148 Forest Road, Tunbridge Wells, Kent TN2 5EY
Telephone 0892 30400

The professional body for herbalists who have been trained in herbal medicine by the Institute's own school. It can provide names and addresses of practising medical herbalists.

British Herbal Medicine Association
The Old Coach House, Southborough Road,
Surbiton, Surrey KT6 6JN
Telephone 01 399 6693

This association exists to protect and promote the interests of manufacturers, practitioners and users of herbal medicine, and publishes the reference book, *The British Herbal Pharmacopoeia.*

Acknowledgement is due to the following
for permission to reproduce illustrations:
A–Z BOTANICAL COLLECTION deadly nightshade, page 76, *Datura stramonium* flower, page 78; BBC HULTON PICTURE LIBRARY elecampane, page 38, feverfew, page 46, periwinkle, page 62; DAI WANG PHARMACEUTICAL CO. LTD. ginseng advertisement, page 13; HARRY SMITH HORTICULTURAL COLLECTION cannabis, page 25, comfrey, page 56 (both K. Rastall), ergot of rye, page 69, opium poppy, page 70, *Datura stramonium* seed pod, page 78 (all Anthony Huxley); THE MANSELL COLLECTION Paracelsus, page 12; KEITH MORRIS Robert Eagle, page 4.

The photograph of Dr. Gorinsky on page 22 was specially taken by Derrick Witty.

The illustrations by Sue Henry, on pages 40, 53, 59, 67 and 74, were specially commissioned.

Acknowledgment is also due to:
THE HOGARTH PRESS LTD for extract from a letter written by Sigmund Freud to his fiancée contained in *The life and work of Sigmund Freud* Vol 1 by Ernest Jones.

Index

Reference to illustrations
are indicated by italic type.